Bureaucracy and World View

Bureaucracy and World View

Studies in the Logic of Official Interpretation

Don Handelman and Elliott Leyton

Social and Economic Studies No. 22

Institute of Social and Economic Research
Memorial University of Newfoundland

Canadian Cataloguing in Publication Data

Main entry under title:

Bureaucracy and world view
(Social and economic studies; no. 22)

Bibliography: p.
ISBN 0-919666-15-9

1. Bureaucracy – Case studies.   2. Civil service –
Newfoundland – Case studies.   3. Public welfare –
Newfoundland – Case studies.   I. Handelman, Don, 1939–
II. Leyton, Elliott, 1939–   III. Memorial University of Newfoundland.
Institute of Social and Economic Research.
IV. Title.   V. Series: Social and economic
studies (St. John's, Nfld.); no. 22.

JL1411.H35   350′.001   C78-001221-6

Printed in Canada by University of Toronto Press

Contents

Acknowledgement

This book has been published with the help of a grant from the Social Science Federation of Canada, using funds provided by the Canada Council.

Preface

Handelman collected his data during 1973–74 while he was a post-doctoral fellow of the Institute of Social and Economic Research.

Handelman wishes to thank in particular Vernon Hollett, Deputy Minister of the Department of Social Services of Newfoundland; Roy Tiller, Director of Field Services; Len Richards of Memorial University; and Myles Hopper, formerly of Memorial University, for greatly easing his path. He is particularly grateful to the regional administrators, supervisors, and welfare officers, who must remain unnamed, but whose active cooperation, interest and friendliness made his work not only possible but also pleasant. The hospitality extended by the Paines, Bravemans, Antlers, Leytons, Jean Briggs, Sterns, and Lazars will not be forgotten; in particular, Av and Marsha Richler provided an ideal ambience for thinking and writing. At the outset of fieldwork, Fred Evans of Memorial University provided valuable advice. Lea Handelman took many hours from her own busy schedule to discuss field data and analysis, and without her logistic and intellectual help this essay would have remained still-born.

All personal names in the text have been changed and some minor details and dates have been altered in an attempt to ensure anonymity. A preliminary version of Handelman's essay was read at an ISER seminar in October 1974. He is indebted to the participants, particularly to Robert Paine and Jean Briggs, for their comments.

Leyton based his analysis on field research conducted in 1974 among the miners' families of St. Lawrence and Lawn, and on additional research in 1975 at the Workmen's Compensation Board in St. John's.

Leyton is indebted to the people of St. Lawrence, Lawn, Lord's Cove, Lorries, and Lamaline for guiding his understanding of their communities; and to the Hon. Frank D. Moores, Premier of Newfoundland; Mr. Ted Blanchard, Deputy Minister of Manpower; and Mr. William May, Chairman of the Workmen's Compensation Board, for their enlightened encouragement of this research. Without their active cooperation, neither the published work nor the report to the Premier would have been possible.

Leyton also expresses his gratitude to the various medical and administrative officials of the Workmen's Compensation Board who helped shape the analysis which follows; their perceptions of the dilemmas of public policy are astute indeed. Special thanks are due to Dr. W. E. Lawton of the Medical Division; Messrs William May, Andrew Rose, and Richard

Fagan of the 'Board'; and Messrs Max Bursey and John Bambrick of the Claims Division. Finally, thanks to Drs. Judith Adler, Gordon Inglis, Ralph Pastore, Stuart Philpott, and George Story for their criticism of various sections of this essay.*

   We both wish to thank Sonia Kuryliw Paine and Jeanette Gleeson for their careful editing and typing of the manuscript, respectively.

Don Handelman   Elliott Leyton
Jerusalem, Israel   Torbay, Newfoundland
July, 1976

---

* It should be pointed out that Alcan shut down permanently the St. Lawrence mines in early 1978 on the grounds that it could obtain cheaper fluorspar from its Mexican sources.

Introduction: A Recognition of Bureaucracy

Don Handelman

COMPENSATION

In 1969 the Royal Commission on radiation, compensation and safety in the St. Lawrence fluorspar mines published its findings on what had become a major industrial disaster: an estimated 150 miners had died and as many as a hundred were permanently disabled by lung cancer, silicosis, and chronic obstructive pulmonary diseases. This was the result of mining operations, which had originally been perceived as a godsend by the impoverished people of the St. Lawrence area. The Royal Commission itself commented that "many witnesses have testified that in those depression days a half-starved man was considered fortunate to hold a job where he could spend ten hours or so each day, drenched in the waters of Black Duck Brook and half choked with dust from his 'hammer' (pneumatic drill), trying to earn enough money to keep his family from starving, in an environment where fuel was just as scarce as food" (1969, p. 33).

The emotive tone of this quotation is unusual in Royal Commission reports, but it reflects the trauma which the disaster exerted upon the people of Newfoundland. Moreover, it exposed the province's Workmen's Compensation Board to intense public scrutiny, and made its compensation practices subject to considerable criticism. Nevertheless, it was not until 1967 that lung cancer was ruled a compensable disease, and not until the Progressive Conservative (PC) Government took office in the 1970s were many of the Royal Commission's recommendations implemented. But the chairman of the Workmen's Compensation Board was clearly moved by the tragedy. In his report to the Royal Commission, he wrote:

The Board could not accept the cases because the Act's Schedule of Industrial Diseases did not include lung cancer, and the statutory definition of industrial diseases precluded consideration of any disease save those listed in the schedule. Why wasn't it included? Because medical science had not caught up with the developing situation! ... In a kind of cumulative disaster, the miners died, one after the other, from lung cancer. Stoic and uncomplaining they went each of them to the grave, leaving a widow and children without means or support. There was no recompense although industry killed them; a strange, uncanny combination of murderous substances, impalpable and invisible, unforeseen and unforseeable, released from the granite bowels of the earth by the industrial process, cut them down. (Royal Commission, 1969:244).

After a careful review of the compensation paid to disabled miners and widows, the commissioners concluded that "it is unjust, humiliating, and degrading for widows of deceased workmen who died as a result of an occupational disease contracted in an industry covered by the Workmen's Compensation Act to be obliged to seek social assistance (welfare) in addition to compensation'' (*op. cit.*:260).

On the basis of this statement, the PC Government made a series of changes in the Compensation Act. Yet inequities continue to exist in St. Lawrence, and the encounter between Compensation Board and miner is still a source of much bitterness. It is the nature of this encounter and the dynamics of perceived injustice that are the focus of the second half of this book.

WELFARE

Towards the end of 1973 the PC Government of Newfoundland published the findings of a Royal Commission inquiry into a welfare client's allegations that in 1971, a former Liberal minister of Social Services had issued her welfare payment after seeing photographs of her in the nude. According to the Commission Report, at a meeting between the minister and representatives of a welfare rights association (also attended by members of the mass media), the client in question ''... stepped forward, kissed the Minister on the cheek and threw seven (7) nude and semi-nude pictures of herself on the Minister's desk. She then charged that the Minister and ... the Director of Social Assistance provided her with Six Hundred Dollars ($600) ... after viewing these nude and semi-nude pictures of herself. She reiterated this charge several times during the meeting and she enlarged upon it immediately after the meeting'' (Royal Commission, 1973:43).[1]

The conjunction of politics, allegations of welfare bureaucracy improprieties, and the public nature of the event itself became of great interest to the people of Newfoundland. A St. John's daily newspaper serialized the text of the report, and accusations and allegations concerning it continued to appear in the mass media – although it probably received little or no exposure outside of Newfoundland.

A few weeks after the report was published, an unsigned editorial appeared in the St. John's daily newspaper, the *Evening Telegram*, commenting on changes in the provincial welfare programme. It stated that the premier ''... is being very naive if he thinks he is going to be successful in his campaign to catch the welfare dodgers. The welfare dodgers are past masters in a philosophy of scrounging which is as old as time itself. They were winning out over authority in the time of Moses and they are still winning.'' A week later, in another unsigned editorial entitled ''The Dark Side,'' the *Evening Telegram* stated:

There is a dark side to living in Newfoundland which the average employed person knows nothing about. The welfare recipient, or the applicant, is the one who knows about it: He knows less than civil treatment from civil servants, gets the feeling that he is a criminal-minded scrounger and is not sure whether he should walk in like a man and demand his rights or should crawl in on hands and knees and beg for mercy.

Most welfare recipients live in fear and dread of the welfare officer. They look on him as the all powerful lord who can give or take away. A frown from the welfare officer is almost the same as a death sentence and few people are brave enough to risk the wrath of these lords of welfare.

At most welfare offices the recipient is treated with less respect than the mat on the floor ... In most areas the welfare officer is lord and master of all he surveys and those who seek his time or attention must put up with his whims, his quirks of personality and any mean or vicious streak that may be included in his character. Most of the people who deal with him treat him with fear rather than respect. They have learned from experience that to make an enemy of the welfare officer is unhealthy and unwise ... Arming civil servants with too much power can be dangerous ... .

Newfoundland has an uncertain industrial base, much seasonal work, a high rate of unemployment, and limited state resources. Within these contexts, a theme which flows through the above excerpts (and numerous others) is an intense interest in, and concern with, the workings of the hidden world of civil service bureaucracy (and particularly the social service bureaucracy), which at one time or another has touched the lives and affected the fates of many Newfoundlanders. Anxieties about the excesses of the 'system' and the indignation over the manoeuverings of its clients are both symptomatic of the centrality of civil bureaucracy in present-day Newfoundland. This location of bureaucracy is not peculiar to Newfoundland, but is an increasingly prominent feature of the social structures of centralizing nation-states.

ANTHROPOLOGY AND BUREAUCRACY

This volume is devoted to exploring aspects of what Schaffer (1975) has termed "the organisational connection" between officials and clients – an interface across which demands are made, requests evaluated, and allocations rendered with consequence. Yet we maintain that bureaucratic organization has been consistently under-studied by anthropology, obscuring our comprehension of how the bureaucratic view – its internal logic of perception and organization – transmutes the interpretation of problems and issues it attends, thereby influencing the decisions it makes. Also hidden are the ways in which intra-societal bureaucratic linkages reinforce the existence of such forms of organization and affirm the form and content of dominant power structures in a given social field.

We, the authors, are social anthropologists who first came upon bureaucratic forms of organization on our way to other destinations.[2] In this there is undoubtedly a lesson about anthropological work, but in quite different settings this process also points out the pervasiveness of bureaucratic forms in social life. Yet, bureaucracy, when it *is* mentioned by anthropologists, is often treated either as an epiphenomenon, a given feature of super-structures, or as an adjunct to the study of other themes. Here, we shall mention two themes within whose contexts the subject of bureaucracy periodically surfaces in anthropological work.

One of these themes is the study of political systems. Geertz (1973:329) has pointed out that the recent study of traditional politics has focused on the foundations and organization of the despotic state, the study of segmentary states, and what he terms "comparative feudalism." In the anthropological treatment of such topics, bureaucratized organization and politicized organization are intimately linked; that is, emphasis is likely to be placed on the political aspects of resource, choice, and decision-making within the moulds of cultural form. Bureaucratic institutions, then, tend to become synonymous with political institutions. Furthermore, although M. G. Smith's (1960) distinction between "systems of political action" and "systems of administrative action" is well known, Swartz (1968:227) indicates that comparatively little attention has been given to the organization of administration in its own right (although Swartz himself argues against the fruitfulness of such a distinction).

The lack of development of this distinction, especially in its organizational sense, is particularly difficult to countenance if one accepts Geertz's (1973:339) argument that a comparison between the ideological contributions to contemporary states of their past cultural traditions and the organizational contributions of past systems of government to present states will show that the former, "... the ideological contribution, is, with some exceptions, of much greater significance than the latter." The adoption of alternative forms of administrative organization, whether at variance with, or adaptable to, traditional forms of ideation, poses as serious analytic problems to students of day-to-day bureaucratic operation as it does to students of politicized behaviour. But we should add the *proviso* that the routine intervention of the bureaucratic process in the lives of citizenry is likely to be a more prominent feature of routine existence in complex societies than is actively politicized behaviour. We shall return to this point later.

The topic of bureaucratic administration also surfaces in anthropological studies of linkages between different strata or segments of a given population through mediating roles which have been variously termed as "inter-calary," "inter-hierarchical" (Gluckman, 1968:71; see also Fallers, 1965), or as brokerage roles (cf. Boissevain, 1974). Thus conceived, although they contain crucial components of administration, inter-hierarchical roles are by definition political since their intent and focus are on the inter-relation of groups or groupings defined as political (that is, the colonizers and the colonized). Thus, strands of administration are also channels of political action for the mediation, suppression, or activation of conflict, instead of being lodged in parallel (although ultimately subordinate) institutions dependent on political winds and will.

Although the middleman function of brokerage roles exists within and between organizations, or between organizations and clienteles, anthropological literature has treated it in a fashion analogous to the idea of "informal organization" in sociology. In both instances the following would appear to be an underlying assumption: since the components of systems, or inter-connections between systems, are imperfectly integrated, and since the channels of communication which would serve such integrative functions are not in operation, persons to whose advantage it is to be in communication will find ways to sidestep or circumvent strictures to establish such connections. Thus the system will acquire a measure of integration, virtually in spite of its own contradictions.

Since the political sector is usually cast in the role of organizer for the overall system (and since the administrative side is frequently underplayed), it is the 'politicized' middleman, or the middleman who earns a 'profit' from political-like activity, upon whom study is focused. To summarize: the concern of political anthropology to uncover dynamics expressive of social structure has resulted in its underplaying of bureaucratic managerial and administrative work, even in societies where political and bureaucratic institutions, although intimately linked, operate apart to an important extent.

Mention of bureaucracy also surfaces from the often-overlapping rubrics of "complex society" and "urban anthropology." The study of linkages between urban and rural locales, which bind territories within the fabric of the nation-state, are often identified as administrative connections. Indeed, Fried (1967:239) argues that the emergence of a bureaucratic sector as a medium of social control is integral to the development and organization of the state. Clearly, among the kinds of connections that articulate territorially defined segments, or that link emergent interest groups to their audiences and to their resource bases (cf. Kapferer, 1972; Grillo, 1973), the bureaucratic connection should be prominent.

The above point is well recognized by anthropologists who are concerned with organizations that transcend or supercede the level of locality. Thus, Leeds makes a case for the examination of "supralocal structures," which he defines as: "... social bodies to whose organizational principles any given set of local and ecological conditions is irrelevant; that is, in their fundamental principles of action, supralocal structures confront any locality, any sociogeographical sub-unit of the total system of its sub-divisions, with uniform, generalized, organizational and operational norms or equipment" (1973:27).

The problem of how supralocal institutions articulate with localities, resource niches, or interest groups has been of interest to anthropologists (cf. Jay, 1969:342–410). However, insufficient attention has been given to the clash between the ways in which supralocal institutions conceive of administrative territories and the ways in which territorially based populations conceive of themselves as communities (cf. Epstein, 1972; Suttles, 1972:44–107). This can be translated, to a significant degree, as the clash between differing definitions of overlapping situations, with each definition supported by a different world of experience, institutional frameworks, resources, and goals. This again brings us to the official/client interface as a crucial point of articulation wherein such discrepancies of connection and communication are most likely to be evident, and hence as a likely node through which to expose the coercion and fragility of structures of power.

The absence of administrative bureaucracy as a focus of anthropological work is indicated further by a perusal of the widely circulated *Biennial Review of Anthropology* and its successor, the *Annual Review of Anthropology*; in no volume is bureaucracy treated as a subject in its own right, or one which can illuminate other aspects of social structure. Instead, references to bureaucratic organization are found in discussions on the *Anthropology of Development* (Rubin, 1962) or *The Anthropology of Complex Society* (Kushner, 1970). As these volumes are compendia of work accomplished, one might expect that the anthropologists who define themselves as "radical" and who are prepared to write programmatic statements of their views would emphasize the importance of studying the bureaucratic connection. In this regard the volume entitled *Reinventing Anthropology* is instructive (Hymes, 1974). Of the sixteen contributors to this volume, only two (Hymes, and Nader) mention bureaucracy as a subject of vital concern to anthropology – this in a book which is intensely concerned with what Berreman terms an "anthropology of experience" (1974:92)[3]. It is obvious that there are serious *lacunae* in the anthropological perception of what is a prime constructor and moulder of 'social reality' in many contemporary societies. This is a selective perception which an anthropology concerned with the structuring of experience, the codification of knowledge, and with the organization of human lives in concert can ill afford.

Given the prominence of bureaucratic organization in the social life of many contemporary societies, where should we go from this realization? We would argue that processes such as state planning, the ideology of welfare statism (concealed beneath a diversity of labels), and the emergence of organized and recognized interest groups have resulted in the burgeoning development of the service sector of bureaucracy: that sector which administers and allocates a diversity of social services to a multitude of different publics, according to the policy directives of politicians. Therefore the service sector deserves more attention by anthropologists; and, without becoming programmatic, a number of areas worthy of detailed examination may be considered:

(a) The decision by persons to establish the organizational connection, to "plug into" bureaucratic organizations as clients, should affect the ways in which they organize their lives in other spheres of existence. Within the simple limitation of time as a resource to be allocated and invested in various settings and social relationships, the establishment of 'clientship' connections will presumably affect the organization and quality of a person's overall social field (cf. Wadel, 1973). How bureaucratic connections influence the reorganization of social fields, the nature of dyadic contracts, the increase or decrease of middleman functions, or the nature of friendship (cf. Paine, 1975:137), are all questions for empirical analysis. How persons who become bureaucratic clients adapt to rules of access, eligibility, evaluation, judgement, and to the nature of benefits received also pose serious questions for analysis (cf. Handelman, 1976).

(b) Schaffer (1972:2) points out that in considering service bureaucracies, it is important to distinguish between the "big programmes" of the organization and its settings, where "... some people want and others are there to give small bits of service." He uses the "queue" as a model for the phased impersonalization and order which culminate in the "... face to face and calculating dyadic situations between the man waiting for service and the man giving it" (*op. cit.*:5). Since officials and clients frequently have different interests at this interface (*op. cit.*:13), the resources introduced to create outcomes are of crucial interest, as are the tactics used to realize such resources. Here officials often have determining advantages since, as Rew points out, "... the queue individuates an access application by dissentangling it from its surrounding social matrix and making it a bureaucratic 'case' to be ordered and dealt with by calculable rules of eligibility" (1975:41). The ways in which dyadic face-to-face contacts between officials and clients can be negotiated to influence outcomes, and the resources and tactics that are introduced into this process are significant problems for analysis.

(c) Although it is the legislators and politicians who establish policies, and what Schaffer terms, the "big programmes," it is the bureaucrat who mediates between legislators and members of the public by interpreting the application of rules to particular cases. (Of course this does not obviate the possibility that persons will approach directly officials higher in the bureaucratic hierarchy than those who face the public, or the policy-makers themselves, but the approach and reaction will be conditioned by the nature of the social field within which such persons exist.) Thus the bureaucrat who deals with the public is not simply an interstitial node of administrative allocation or of information-transmission who functions in a mechanical fashion, but rather, he is an active contributor to the production of decisions, the application of rule to case. The mediating aspects of official roles, whether they be in the tradition of brokerage or whether they apply to the relevance of different rules to the perception of a particular case, should be a central focus of research – in particular, how policies are translated into practice.

(d) Associated with the problems of negotiation and mediation are 1) the ways and the situations in which the state can intervene in the lives of its citizenry through its component service organizations; 2) the bases of legitimation for such intervention; and 3) the intended and unintended consequences of such intervention (cf. Platt, 1969; Kay, 1969). The socio-historical emergence of categories of persons and activities over which service bureaucracies have rights in the name of the state is a prominent feature of present-day societal landscapes and a linch-pin in the social construction of these realities.

That service bureaucracies have acquired rights to intervene in matters which, in simpler societies, are frequently handled within kinship networks is implicit in both essays in this volume. That such intervention often marks major discontinuities between bureaucratic intention and actual effect is an important point in Leyton's essay. Why I chose to examine cases of child neglect and abuse is because they are clearly instances of intervention in the name of service. Moreover, such instances dramatize and emphasize the scale of the processes of interpretation which, I suggest, are integral to the bureaucratic process as a human enterprise. In this I am influenced by Lee's (1950) discussion of lineal and non-lineal codifications of reality.[4]

Bureaucratic perception and interpretation are closely connected to the existence of social categories and constructs which bind such processes, and which are legitimated largely by government policies in present-day states. Thus, bureaucratic perceptions, as well as bureaucratic institutions, support the power structures of the state as do frequently client perceptions of bureaucracy.[5]

(e) Mention should also be made here of the importance of uncovering the 'logic' of bureaucratic organizations; this theme is prominent in both essays. Emphasis is placed on the perceptions of officials within the context of their organizations, including not only the socio-cultural categories by which they are constrained to work, but also the structural effects of organizational infrastructures, of webs of social relationships, and ideas on their perceptions and freedom of action. Frequently such structural effects are latent properties of organization (namely, bureaucratic "ritualism" resulting from what Merton terms "goal displacement," discussed in Blau and Meyer, 1971:100–05).

An excellent example of this occurrence is found in Blumberg (1970). Blumberg discusses how the structure of relationships in an American criminal court, a bureaucratic organization, subverts the ideology of the adversary system of legal process wherein the legal defender should be committed first and foremost to his client's welfare, in opposition to the prosecutor, with the judge serving as an impartial arbiter. Instead, the structure of the relationships is such that judge, prosecutor, and defender frequently work together as members of an organization through which clients simply pass on; and hence, clients are perceived as most peripheral to the continuity and stability of the organization and to the social relationships which develop between its more permanent members. Consequently, judge, prosecutor, and defender often act as a cabal to deprive defendants of their best possible defence, and to keep the queue of clients moving at a proper pace. This is a most significant point which should be examined in the operation of service bureaucracies, since in them the client (the overt purpose of service allocation and intervention) is the most peripheral and transitory feature of an otherwise comparatively stable organizational landscape. The accomplishment of client turnover, therefore, may imply applications of bureaucratic perception and logic that are more compatible with the structure of an organization than with the goals it was founded to meet, or than with the ideology supplied to organization members to enable them to focus their attentions on such goals.

In approaching the subject of bureaucracy, anthropologists would do well to recognize the changing treatment which sociologists have given the subject. Although Rew is correct in criticizing a sociology of organizations that "... has been oriented to the definition of the situation held by the higher levels of the organization, viewing deviations from that definition as a deficit to be sanctioned, adjusted and manipulated into more manageable forms" (1975:39), developments have occurred which require the serious attention of anthropology.

In his discussion of post-Weberian theories of bureaucracy, Mouzelis raises three points of interest. Instead of conceiving of the bureaucrat as a stick figure, "a mere administrative tool," he recognizes him "... as a whole human being with emotions, beliefs and goals ... which do not always coincide with the general goals of the organization" (1969:57), but which can affect the operation of the organization. In other words, although not necessarily phrased in these terms, the bureaucrat as interpreter, mediator, and negotiator is no longer insensitive to sociological perspectives; furthermore an understanding of bureaucratic work requires the analysis of social relationships between officials, between officials and clients, and of the more inclusive social fields within which contacts and relationships are played out. Mouzelis' second point of interest to us is the cessation of conceiving bureaucracy "... to be merely a formal arrangement of consciously coordinated activities," but instead conceiving of bureaucratic organization as a social system, "... a system which is partly shaped by purposive design and partly formed spontaneously by forces emerging during the interaction of social beings" (*op. cit.*:58). However, it is not a social system which has solved its structural problems and the nature of its relations with the wider social fields within which it exists. Instead (Mouzelis' third point of interest), there is ongoing tension between rules which are intended to control the behaviours of system members and between "... the 'recalcitrance' of such behavior which defies full control and develops in an unpredicted manner, and which generates new situations and needs which in their turn bring forth a renewed attempt to control the situation by further rules" (*op. cit.*:60). Thus, there is an inherent dialectic in bureaucratic relationships between formal rules and social situations that generates changes in both spheres. Although these points have a functionalist cast, other sociological work on bureaucratic organizations has begun to fill a vital gap in the interaction between rules and their application to social situations.

In order for rules to be applied to social situations (namely, to 'cases'), one must know how officials perceive these rules and how they conceive of the persons who approach them as clients. In other words, one must know the 'native' conceptions of social categories and social situations. With the identification of such socio-cognitive resources within the process of interpretation, it then becomes possible to uncover the dynamics of the application of rule to case. It makes little sense for the officials to ask only "what kind of case is this?" since the categorization of *case* is often intimately related to questions of "what kind of person is this?" and "what rules apply?" or can be made to apply. Hence the typification of client, problem, rule-eliciting situation, and thus case, influences the bureaucratic perception and interpretation of rules, thereby influencing bureaucratic decisions and outcomes.

'Native' conceptions of person, place, and problem mediate the application of rule to case; but these conceptions are not simply products of certain sets of rules. Instead they are the products of complex interactions among the cultural, organizational, and cognitive components of the social fields within which bureaucracy is located. That sociology is producing work in which native (namely, bureaucratic) conceptions demonstrably influence the ways in which bureaucratic organizations operate is evident in empirical research on welfare (Zimmerman, 1969; Scott, 1969) and on the legal process (Sudnow, 1965; Cicourel, 1968; Emerson, 1969; Bittner, 1967), among other subjects. We would argue that certain current directions in the sociological study of bureaucratic organizations are much more compatible with anthropological work than perhaps has been appreciated.

Nevertheless, in all of this discussion of bureaucracy, there remains the question (and in turn the question of whether such a query is relevant) of whether there are themes which are peculiarly anthropological. In our view the extent of overlap between anthropology and neighbouring disciplines is substantial. Still, one can point to new directions of promise. For instance, if cross-cultural motifs are used, not as simple glosses for complex realities, but to investigate the interdependencies and discontinuities between cultural forms and institutional structures (cf. Kiefer, 1970), then such subjects remain consistent with anthropological endeavour; and the obvious value of detailed studies of bureaucratic organizations in different societies will remain the bedrock for a comparative anthropology in such spheres. In concluding his recent study of a Japanese bank, Rohlen writes (and we echo) that there are obvious transcultural similarities between forms of modern organizations. Yet, "... these uniformities have been so apparent, it seems, that anthropologists have shied from the subject on the assumption that it is infertile ground for their inherent concern with cultural difference. I feel that no better territory exists for such exploration, particularly since other social sciences have made so much of late about the eclipse of cultural differences that modernization brings" (1974:270).

With their concern for cultural difference, anthropologists have often tried to discover the 'inside view' held by actors in different social niches. The logic of cognition, perception, and interpretation appear to be rooted in world views. Whatever the nature of world views (and we suggested earlier that discovering them was of vital importance), they appear to be conditioned contextually by the logic of operation of bureaucratic organizations whose mandates often cross-cut the boundaries of community, locality, class, and ethnicity, and so affect different people in different ways. Thus the bureaucrats' decisions reverberate beyond the confines of his place of work.

Hence the anthropologist has a particular mandate to inquire into the nature of bureaucratic experience: into the interplay between guidelines of cultural codes and the flexibility of the individual life-world of experience within the context of organizational forms (cf. Rohlen, 1974; Taub, 1969). We would suggest that if the anthropologist were concerned with the effects of bureaucracy on client populations, then a natural area of study would be that of service bureaucracy and the official/client interface. Such an interface immediately brings to mind interlocking social fields of different scale and quality. And the inclusion of such fields, as modifying contexts within which organizations operate, would have a salutory effect on some sociological trends which, too often, depict the organization as – to borrow an aphorism from Ashley Montagu – "a womb with a view."

To carry out such a task, anthropological methods are most apt. If we value the data of observation and encounter, why should we be content to attribute ideal-type characteristics to bureaucrats and to bureaucracy (as so much sociological work still does), and then to treat these as givens or constants in accordance with the assumptions of their attribution? It is only through the observation of people at work, of the nuances of transaction between officials and clients, that the reality of bureaucracy can be depicted. Moreover, an anthropological concern with diachronic perspectives of social events, and a concern for the history of social relationships as they relate to present encounters can be richly realized (although often unevenly) through the use of bureaucratic records.[6]

Moreover, anthropology has the potential to shed light on aspects of bureaucracy that, to the best of our knowledge, have remained untreated by the social sciences. One such area is bureaucracy and bureaucrat as societal symbols. To borrow from a concern of Victor Turner's, what are the "root metaphors" of bureaucracy in a particular society? We would suggest, as a working hypothesis, that in modern industrialized societies the bureaucrat is a prime symbol of "structure," of order, as against societal symbols of "communitas" (see Turner, 1974), or symbols that can be infused with communitas. The archtypal bureaucrat categorizes divides, and individualizes a populace; hence the symbolism of bureaucracy identifies with the structure of the state. But on the other hand such symbolism mediates against an isomorphism of communitas sentiments, of equality and solidarity, with the boundaries of the state as a social unit. Furthermore, in comparison with other archtypal figures who have contact with the public (for example, the politician, the mass media personage, the religious personage), the bureaucrat is the least likely to have access to symbols of communitas, and hence, is the least likely to have opportunities to manipulate such symbols. Thus, for example, the terms of the opposition bureaucrat/politician suggest a good reason for not identifying wholly the study of bureaucracy with the study of political process, a point touched on earlier in this discussion.

Whereas other archetypal figures can manipulate symbols to move between the poles of structure and anti-structure, the bureaucrat cannot (so long as he remains one). This attribute of symbolic immutability ensures that bureaucracy will stand for the order of a complex division of labour, a particular system of ownership, and the rights of the state. On the other hand, again because of this symbolic immutability, the bureaucrat is highly vulnerable should sentiments of mass solidarity be turned against him, since his base can only negate such communitas-like sentiments and is therefore vulnerable to its mass opposition. This raises interesting questions about the role of bureaucracy in times of social change, particularly change that is ignited by mass movements. And one may wonder about the symbolic and organizational oppositions between phases in the process of the institutionalization of change. In considering these questions we are made aware of the fragility of bureaucratic stability in the face of a mass movement marked by strong sentiments of equality and solidarity, such as the Cultural Revolution, the symbols of which were directed, in part, against those of the bureaucratic order in accordance with the manipulative goals of politicians (cf. Ling, 1972).

Thus, it is in a spirit of exploration, and with a firm conviction that anthropologists should take upon themselves the study of bureaucracy that the essays in this volume are offered. We believe, as well, that this task will be enhanced if ideas and research from other disciplines are incorporated. That the bureaucratic connection is prominent in Newfoundland we have no doubt, although a more detailed exposition of its operation, particularly that dealing with public welfare, will have to await future publication.

We also hope that this volume will encourage the reader to devote more thought to the bureaucratic process.

NOTES

1   The Report completely exonerated the ex-Minister and the Director of Social Assistance from these allegations. But it did uncover procedural irregularities in the granting of services to the client and her husband, who in their turn were found to have obtained fraudulently welfare monies by altering social assistance cheques.

2   Leyton recognized the significance of the WCB during his study of miners disabled by industrial disease and of their widows in the Newfoundland community of St. Lawrence (Leyton, 1975). Handelman recognized the significance of the 'welfare connection' in shaping the life-lines of these persons in a study of elderly indigents employed in sheltered workshops in Jerusalem (1971, 1976, n.d.). As an aside we might note that in Israel – a highly bureau-cratized society – anthropologists have consistently found it a prerequisite to take into account factors of bureaucracy in their analysis, regardless of the ways in which they defined the social units which they investigated, whether it was the effects of state marketing boards and controlled water quotas in farming communities (cf. Baldwin, 1972), or the adaptation of new immigrants to planned farming communities (cf. Weingrod, 1966; Shokeid, 1971; Willner, 1969), or the organization and distribution of housing, work, and welfare in urban com-munities (cf. Marx, 1973; Aronoff, 1974).

3   Nader (1974:292–93) writes: "It is appropriate that a reinvented anthropology should study powerful institutions and bureaucratic organizations in the United States, for such institutions and their network systems affect our lives and also affect the lives of people that anthropologists have traditionally studied all around the world." We agree wholeheartedly with this position.

4   Most of Handelman's time in Newfoundland was devoted to observing contacts in office settings between welfare officers and public welfare recipients. Although the range and scale of interpretations in such cases were different from those involved in child neglect and abuse, the quality of interpretations would be similar. Leyton's research consisted of interviews in the St. Lawrence area together with the observation of interaction and the study of files at the WCB offices in St. John's in order to ascertain the criteria officials used to interpret St. Lawrence cases.

5   This is put well by Blau and Meyer (1971:151): "Fuming against red tape and bureaucratic methods serves as a psychological substitute for opposition to bureaucratic policies that

violate the interests of individuals. The fact that frustration is expressed in accusations of inefficiency, rather than in opposition to policies indicates how powerful bureaucracies are.''
6   One problem that fieldworkers who study bureaucratic organizations have to overcome is obtaining permission to enter the organization for research purposes. On the other hand, once permission is forthcoming, compared with research situations in many communities, neighbourhoods, and so forth, the researcher is usually free to pursue his investigations openly. Regarding the collection of data presented in this volume, Leyton had to receive permission from the Premier of Newfoundland, and Handelman from the Minister of Social Services before fieldwork could begin.

Bureaucratic Interpretation: The Perception of Child Abuse in Urban Newfoundland

2

Don Handelman

INTRODUCTION

In his exposition of the rational-legal bureaucratic type of organization, Weber (1964:330) wrote that: "... every body of law consists essentially in a consistent system of abstract rules which have normally been intentionally established. Furthermore, administration of law is held to consist in the application of these rules to particular cases." Later he added: "Bureaucratic administration means fundamentally the exercise of control on the basis of knowledge. This is the feature which makes it specifically rational ... they [officials] acquire through the conduct of office a special knowledge of facts and have available a store of documentary material peculiar to themselves" (p. 339). In these passages Weber touched on two focal aspects of the daily life of bureaucratic organization: the "special knowledge" with which officials typify the elements of a particular instance, and the relevance of these typifications in the application of rule to case. Such typifications are intermediate constructions of reality, often uncodified, which mediate between the "stock of knowledge" (Schutz and Luckmann, 1973:99ff) of protagonists, including their knowledge of organizational rules and the elements of a particular instance. Since such typifications are always problem-oriented (Schutz and Luckmann, 1973:231), the application of rule to case is often problematic, in the sense that, consciously or unconsciously, the connectiveness between stock of knowledge and particular instance must be established, such that the instance becomes a representation of a type of instances. The protagonists must interpret the elements of the instance according to what they decide are the relevant aspects of their stock of knowledge in order to make sense of the instance as official work. Therefore a major task of the student of bureaucracy is to try to uncover the 'common-sense' assumptions used by officials as they apply their stock of knowledge to the interpretation of instances in order to make these instances intelligible in the light of the organizational life-world within which they work.

This paper proceeds on the assumption that the stock of knowledge of organization members offers typified schemes for the interpretation of a particular instance (see Bittner, 1965) that are deemed relevant to the concerns of the organization, such that the decision governing the instance is rendered intelligible to, and compatible with, the life-world of the organization (cf. Silverman and Jones, 1973).

Instances of suspected child neglect or abuse in urban Newfoundland make the process of typification and interpretation particularly problematic. An event is presumed to have occurred (without necessarily specifying an underlying pattern of causality and motivations at this point) which may be finally (in terms of the disposition of the case at the time of decision) decided upon as child neglect and/or abuse. The child-welfare worker in charge of the case has at his/her disposal a number of legal criteria according to which he/she must demonstrate the correctness of his/her decision for the organization. He/she also has at his/her command a number of decision categories within which to dispose of the case upon arriving at a decision. But the rules or guidelines of the organization do not specify how a child-welfare worker is to decide which decision category is applicable to the instance. Since he/she must reach a decision within a fairly short period, "The process of explication must be pushed on ahead until determinations are found in the theme (the instance or event) which are compatible with the interpretively relevant determination ..." (Schutz and Luckmann, 1973:206). Thus the child-welfare worker must proceed from event to decision with a stock of officially uncodified knowledge that is based on certain common-sense assumptions about the motivation and character of his/her clients, and about the settings and contexts of their displayed behaviour, in order to decide 'what really happened.' 'What happened' is then a function of the "investigative stance" (Zimmerman, 1969) adopted by the worker in order to construct a story-line intelligible to, and justifiable in terms of the organizational goals and conditions of his/her employment. There may well be other versions of 'what really happened' that remain relevant to contexts other than the bureaucratic one (cf. Cicourel, 1973:124).

The above is not meant to suggest that the stock of knowledge, and hence typifications, of each child-welfare worker in the organization are idiosyncratic expressions of his/her particular social biography, although the perceptions of each worker will certainly be affected by it. For, as Jehenson (1973:226) suggests, "... the assignment of meaning is not left to the discretion of the member. The organization presents him with a number of anonymous, functional typifying schemes that will help him orient his behavior ... By such standardization of the scheme of typifications, the organization attempts to establish a congruency between the typified scheme by each actor as a scheme of orientation and that of his organizational fellow-men as a scheme of interpretation ..." (see also Smith, 1974:265). Thus, although a particular instance need not be perceived as problematic by an official but rather as a version of "normal trouble"

(Sudnow, 1965), the search for 'what really happened' still proceeds in the manner outlined by Schutz and Luckmann (1973:207). "In general, the structure of interpretational relevance is determined by the principle of compatibility: compatibility between the current theme (its determinations that are presented as 'typical') and the interpretational schemata in the stock of knowledge." They continue: "The problem requiring explication is interpreted, in that what thematically is actually brought into relief is 'compared' with the 'available' elements of knowledge ('results' of the interpretation of earlier problems) themselves ... The interpretation may be pursued until the unfamiliar is sufficiently familiar ..." (*op. cit.*:225). Moreover, even in the pursuit of the routinely familiar, those elements of knowledge and typifications which are unequivocally relevant or irrelevant will represent only marginal cases. "... interpretational relevance has a 'more or less' character" (*op. cit.*:201).

This paper is concerned with the analysis of interpretations made by officials in St. John's, Newfoundland in the course of attempting to unravel the facts of a case which came to be termed "child abuse." The presentation is that of the extended-case method (Van Velsen, 1967) used in social anthropology. This method has a number of advantages: 1) By presenting the case as it developed through a number of phases, the emergent and sometimes changing stands of the protagonists can be uncovered with greater accuracy; 2) As new items of information come to the attention of officials during the development of the case, one can evaluate how they influenced the officials' thinking; 3) The method provides a key to perceiving how the sphere of relevance of certain kinds of knowledge expands and contracts in apparent response to situational demands as officials attempt to typify the case. Then one may be able to specify also whether the common-sense assumptions introduced by officials are those of the stock of knowledge of the organization, or of the wider life-worlds of officials, and the extent to which the bureaucratic and wider life-worlds are interpenetrated in the realm of knowledge; 4) The idea of *case* would appear to be an emic conception for child-welfare workers, thereby perhaps establishing a more valid connection between the child-welfare worker's investigation of the case and the researcher's inquiry into a unit of analysis with analogous boundaries.

The reader will be introduced to the development of a typification, the "battered-child syndrome," which forms part of the occupational stock of knowledge of child-welfare workers, affecting their perception of instances of suspected abuse or neglect. Following the delineation of this typification, the reader will be introduced to aspects of the urban and organizational contexts that affect the processing of instances of suspected abuse/neglect in St. John's. These two sections, then, will indicate elements of the occupational and organizational life-worlds of the child-welfare worker as they are contained within his/her stock of knowledge, and so are available for the interpretation of particular instances.

THE PERCEPTION OF CHILD ABUSE

Child neglect/abuse in North America began to be recognized as an official category of concern for the helping professions and for the law only after the Mary Ellen case of 1866, when the American Society for the Prevention of Cruelty to Animals proved to be the only agency capable of intervention in an instance of child abuse (Zalba, 1971:60). The case resulted in the formation of the Society for the Prevention of Cruelty to Children. This and other rescue societies were intended to provide protection for "dependent" children, and to initiate the prosecution of parents and other adults who neglected or mistreated children (Platt, 1969:108). Various institutions were developed in nineteenth-century America to cope with the placement and rehabilitation of neglected and delinquent children. This trend culminated in the founding of the juvenile court system which established the primacy of the state in the processing and control of children deemed neglected, abused, or delinquent. The child-saving movements created the new role of social worker, and "... child saving was further legitimized by the rising influence of a professional class of correctional administrators who developed medical-therapeutic strategies for controlling and reforming 'delinquent' youth" (Platt, 1969:177).

During the past fifty years the development of psychoanalysis, psychiatry, and clinical psychology have provided the legitimacy for, and techniques of therapeutic intervention within the family on the part of the helping professions. Because of its reliance on these approaches, social work, including child work, has directed much of its efforts to delineating and changing the personality structures and motivations of its clients (cf. Greenaway, 1973). Within public-welfare agencies this emphasis has probably been more true for child-welfare divisions than for social-assistance departments, since child workers were relatively free of the stricture to guard the public purse against the sallies of the welfare client. But, except in extreme cases, child-welfare workers have found it difficult to establish conceptual connections between typifications of the personalities of suspected child-abusers and the physical symptoms exhibited by their children. In the western tradition of valuing 'hard' science, medical diagnoses have tended to prevail over clinical diagnoses in influencing juvenile or family courts; and medical evaluations have tended to emphasize the individual injuries of the child, rather than his or her overall condition.

The verification of instances of child abuse, particularly among infants, received greater legitimacy in 1946 when the radiologist, Caffey, reported a correlation between certain fractures in the long bones and subdural hematomas. Subsequent radiological evidence indicated that such lesions were traumatic in origin, and deliberately inflicted in some cases. In 1962 the identification of child abuse was eased once again when the pediatrician Kempe (Kempe *et al*:1962) constructed the "battered-child syndrome," which subsumed a number of physical and behavioural characteristics suggesting abuse. The importance of the construction of such a gloss cannot be overemphasized in providing child-welfare workers with a typification that purported to identify abuse, although its criteria existed only in association. This is evident in the pediatrician, Helfer's, conception of what constitutes an "indefinite case." "It is the indefinite case such as an isolated subdural hematoma without a history of trauma, fracture, or bruising that poses a difficult problem. ... Children with extensive ecchymoses and no other physical findings also present a difficult diagnostic problem" (Helfer, 1974:29). The unclear instance, then, is one which cannot be easily subsumed within a more comprehensive diachronic or synchronic typification. That such typifications are elastic will be considered shortly.

Even when medical experts maintain that injuries caused by childbattering are quite specific, there remain aspects which can be clarified only through references to typified behaviours or social contexts. Thus Silverman, a radiologist who helped determine diagnostic criteria of the battered-child syndrome, writes:

Although they [the child's injuries] may reflect the time of injury with considerable accuracy and permit extremely accurate deductions concerning the nature of the forces producing the injury, they provide no information whatsoever concerning the circumstances surrounding the injury or the motivation of the individuals responsible. The epiphyseal separation which results from grabbing the child by a limb to prevent a serious fall is indistinguishable from the epiphyseal separation incurred while the infant is being vigorously shaken or otherwise abused by an irate, distraught adult custodian. The recognition of the radiographic changes, however, does constitute a distinct indication to investigate the circumstances surrounding the injury (1974:58; see also pp. 51, 56).

The forensic pathologist, Weston (1974:85), echoes these cautions regarding the difficulty in establishing contradictions between accounts of fatal injuries and pathological findings in order to establish physical abuse.

Where medical personnel might point to an instance of suspected childbattering, interpreted according to criteria that arouse suspicion, those personnel who officially had to process and treat the families concerned had different priorities of relevance. Given their ideologies of therapeutic intervention and legal protection, they were required to construct cases which dealt not with associations, but with cause-and-effect, in order to allocate responsibility for the instance (which could affect the legal disposition of the case), and to establish why the instance had occurred (which could affect the course of rehabilitation decided upon).[1] Inevitably a shift in focus occurred from the abused child to the abusing parents. Perhaps just as inevitably, the typifications which were introduced to explain the causality of abuse were psychological ones.

But the clinical constructs of abuse as cause-and-effect rested heavily on the medical construct of abuse as a syndrome of attributes which coincided in association with one another. Thus the approach of the clinician, or 'intervenor,' was to accept that children, identified as abused according to the syndrome, came from families with one or more child-abusers, and then to treat such persons as if they were indeed persons who abused their children. So Steele and Pollock (1974:90), in a pioneering study of therapeutic intervention, noted that they began by treating parents of children with severe injuries only. But, "Soon we became aware that we were dealing only with the extreme of a much more widespread phenomenon and began including cases in which the infant was moderately bruised by severe hitting, shaking, yanking, choking, or being thrown about."

While Steele and Pollock admit to the difficulty of separating cases of injury caused by brutality from those resulting from disciplinary punishment, one of the tenets of therapeutic intervention is to oppose corporal punishment in principle, and to regard its use as evidence that the perpetrators are beset by psychological problems. Clearly such an approach raises a host of problems of definition and typification. Given a normal distribution of modes of physical contact in play, horseplay, fights between children, discipline, and brutality, the majority of cases which would come to the attention of officials and intervenors might well be instances of light or moderate injuries (cf. Gil, 1973:119). If these instances were to be treated as suspected abuse, or as abuse, the parents involved could then be treated as if they suffered from certain inadequacies or psycho-pathologies. *Ad absurdum*, officials might find themselves stating that parents should be forbidden to strike their children under any circumstances, as occurred in the case to be analysed.

In setting the initial medical delineation of abuse within a motivational matrix, clinicians and social workers were creating a construct which enabled them to fulfill their professional tasks of uncovering psychological causes in order to propose solutions that fell within their sphere of competence. For example, Davoren (1974:136) states that: "The most outstanding characteristic the child beaters share is their attitude toward their children. Understanding this attitude and what it means helps one to *make sense* [my emphasis] of the behavior of these people." Here the invocation of the psychological construct of *attitude* is used to define a population of child-beaters, which is then searched for evidence of the typicality they are presumed to possess. Since child-beaters are a typified population to begin with, they would undoubtedly be found to possess those psychological attributes which the official or clinician attributes to such a typification.

In other words, an ideological typification is invoked to define a population which is then expected to exhibit evidence in support of the typification. When such support is forthcoming, as it usually is within the labyrinth of clinical reasoning, it is not treated as one approximation of the reality of the situation, but as *the* reality which enables the helper to make sense of the child-beater because it is *the* reality that is imbedded in this person, and which caused him to behave in a pathological manner.[2] Thus the professional's stock of knowledge provides explanations that override and subsume the reality of the client's life-world by denying its relevance, and by replacing it with a reality which has greater meaning for the official or professional in the conduct of his routine tasks. Whether a parent is a child-abuser, and to what extent, remains in many cases a matter of official typification and disposition.

The ideological accretion of motivational structure as explanation also allows professionals to begin to de-emphasize the significance of physical symptoms, and instead to stress their underlying causes. For example, Gil, in a major study of the epidemiology and etiology of child abuse, maintains that previous attempts to define this phenomenon produced vague and ambiguous statements. He attributes this in part to: "... definitions of child abuse in terms of the observed effects of an attack on a child, such as injuries sustained by him, rather than in terms of the motivation and behavior of the attacking person" (Gil, 1970:5–6). Instead he offers a definition of physical abuse built almost entirely on "... the intentional, nonaccidental use of physical force ... aimed at hurting, injuring, or destroying that child." He states further that, in practice, instances of abuse may involve a complex mixture of intentional and accidental elements which are difficult to separate.[3] Like "attitude," "intention," in its conscious and unconscious aspects, remains a psychological construct highly amenable to tailoring on the part of experts (cf. Scott, 1970).

The final step in the reconstitution of child abuse in the image of clinicians and welfare workers occurs when the expert can elevate the psychological 'symptoms' of the abusing parent, and their motivational causes, to the same level of validation as that of the medical aspects of the battered-child syndrome. Thus Morris and Gould (1963:32) state that: "The etiology of this syndrome is essentially social [read psychological] – and social and relationship symptoms are *as clear* as medical symptoms. Moreover, they are *always* present, even when bruises and broken bones are not" [my emphasis]. In this way the typification of child abuse has become not merely elastic, but an open-ended construct which validates the continual accretion of new attributes of abuse to encompass a growing client population which only the expert is qualified to process and treat in accordance with his self-definition of competence, and in accordance with his own professional definitions of relevance and causation. As Gelles (1974:193) has pointed out, most of the adherents of what he terms the "psychopathological model" of child abuse "make a special effort to point out that social variables *do not* [his emphasis] enter into the causal scheme of child abuse."[4]

The full-blown battered-child syndrome includes the following kinds of elements:

(1) Multiple skeletal injuries, in different phases of healing.
(2) Accompanying multiple soft tissue injuries.
(3) Correlation between subdural hematoma and long bone injuries.
(4) A delay in bringing the child for treatment.
(5) Parental accounts of the injury which do not coincide with clinical findings.
(6) "Evasion" and "unexplained contradictions" in parental accounts of how the injury occurred.
(7) The parents usually do not freely offer explanations of the child's injury to hospital personnel.
(8) When parents are questioned they are usually evasive and tend to contradict themselves in describing the circumstances of the injury.
(9) "... they seem irritated at being asked for symptoms."
(10) They are angry at the child for becoming injured, and show no "guilt" or "remorse."
(11) The parents appear unconcerned about the nature of the injury, its treatment, and the prognosis of the child.
(12) They often leave the hospital while the child is being admitted.
(13) They tend not to visit the child in the hospital.
(14) When they do visit the child they rarely touch him or look at him.
(15) The parents do not inquire about the child's expected date of discharge, or about follow-up care. (The above criteria are taken from Morris and Gould, 1963).

Morris and Gould then suggest that, "While any one of the reactions listed for the neglecting, battering parents is a danger signal, almost all of them [criteria 7–15] are usually concurrently evident" (p. 40). Other criteria focus on the behaviour of the child. If the child appears overly quiet, withdrawn, frightened of being touched or handled, and prefers not to see one or both parents, the suspicions of hospital personnel are to be aroused. (These criteria and the above list are not meant to be comprehensive, since official personnel continue to add criteria to develop a more definitive syndrome.)

One may well ask how hospital personnel and social workers are able to perceive evasion, contradiction, the free offering of information, irritation, anger, guilt, remorse and unconcern, and other such criteria which lead them to believe that the child has been abused. Such criteria (4–15) appear to be a combination of clinical constructs and common-sense assumptions about how typical parents of a typical child of a given age would behave in the full knowledge of the medical and psychological consequences of whatever has befallen the child. Clearly parents are expected to behave as officials would expect them to behave, given the occupational and professional concerns of the officials involved. Having established criteria of relevance, officials then evaluate deviation as suspicious. Moreover, officials evaluate such deviation (rather than variation) as necessarily significant, that is, symptomatic of the problem that they have to decipher. Therefore they treat such criteria as symptomatic of a 'real' problem that exists within the household, rather than a problem that is made real by their own organizational and occupational tasks.

Put simply, the story-line which they construct about "what happened" is predicated largely upon professional, organizational, and official conceptions of relevance, and how these are to be interpreted. In the main, alternative accounts of what happened, for example from the parents' perspective, are not considered as relevant. As Schutz and Luckmann have pointed out, relevance is problem-oriented; and the nature of the problem, its causes and its solutions, are constructed and imbued with meaning by professional and official persons.[5]

Therefore the kinds of criteria listed previously are not simply *ad hoc* renderings of the relevance of inferences based on certain kinds of evidence. Presumably they represent organized and coherent typifications of certain kinds of persons that legitimize investigation, which in turn uncovers causal factors substantiating the relevance of the initial suspicions generated by the initial perception of medical and behavioural criteria. Although such reasoning is teleological in structure, its circularity is rendered linear by the assumption that it is "really" a cause-and-effect relationship which is being uncovered. Furthermore, this is not a closed system of interconnections since the nature of behavioural attributes and of psychological constructs of first causes permit, and indeed, encourage the continual accretion of additional attributes. This serves the function of developing a more comprehensive conception of syndrome, and of developing psychological (or other) theories of causation that generate the expression of behavioural attributes. This may be the essence of the social construction of reality as it pertains to official understandings and to official explanations of particular instances.

The purpose of this section is to indicate certain problematic aspects in the development of the notion of child abuse – problematic not in the sense of being invalid, but rather that the perceived reality of abuse is constructed in conjunction with the ideologies and tasks of those persons who evaluate and process the cases, and according to the kinds of typifications outlined in this section. Establishing an instance as abuse is often problematic, the typification of the proposed cause of abuse is problematic, and the relationship between instance, decision, and suggested cause is problematic.

My delineation of the perceptions of child abuse has been general and has oversimplified differences in orientations between schools of thought. However, this generality assumes specificity in the mind of a child-welfare worker; selective parts of his stock of knowledge are made relevant to a worker when he must interpret and evaluate a particular instance. The variable of relevance itself is a function of the particular organization that employs the worker, the kinds of accounts which must be produced to meet the criteria of the organization and of other audiences, and the particular setting of which the instance is a part. I now consider briefly aspects of the organizational processing of suspected instances of child abuse in St. John's, Newfoundland.

THE PROCESSING OF CHILD ABUSE

The district office of the Department of Social Services is located on the fringe of the old inner city of St. John's. Sections of the old city have a high proportion of single-detached or semi-detached dwellings, boarding houses, and rooming houses. Many of the dwellings are small, the streets they front on are narrow, and persons have relatively high acoustic or visual access to the lives of others, whether within or between dwellings.

Most of the instances of suspected neglect/abuse that come to the attention of the Child Welfare Division are located in this area of the city. During August through October 1974, of 44 suspected instances, 6 (14%) were located approximately one-tenth of a mile from the district office, 28 (60%) were located within five-tenths of a mile, and 36 (82%) within one mile of the office. Only six instances were located completely outside the inner city. Of these, two were suburban and one was rural.[6]

It is difficult to establish, on the basis of population distribution, whether child abuse is concentrated in particular areas of the city; however, statistics indicate that this is the case. Sixty percent of suspected instances were located within five-tenths of a mile of the district office. This radius cuts through parts of census tracts 5, 6, 7, 10, and 11, which have a combined population of 35, 315, or 27 percent of the metropolitan population of 131, 810 (Statistics Canada, 1973). As a crude estimate, approximately some 21,000 persons lived within those portions of census tracts 5, 6, 7, 10, and 11 which fell within the area of five-tenths of a mile radius around the district office. Thus approximately 16 percent of the metropolitan population contained 60 percent of reported instances of suspected neglect/abuse during August-October 1974.

Instances of suspected neglect/abuse are always brought to the attention of the child-welfare authorities, and it is mandatory for child workers to investigate every report, regardless of its source. The Child Welfare Act of Newfoundland, 1972, makes the reporting of suspected neglect/abuse mandatory (Article 49, Subsection 1); and "... no action lies against the informant unless the giving of the information is done maliciously or without reasonable and probable cause" (Article 49, Subsection 2).[7] Maliciousness and reasonable and probable cause remain undefined, and to my knowledge no informant has ever been prosecuted on these grounds. In the initial phase of an investigation, no distinction is made between the kinds of sources that report information. Reports or complaints are made either directly to the Department of Social Services or to the police, who then refer the case to the department. The thirty-eight cases which I examined contained eighty-nine references to reports or complaints regarding suspected neglect/abuse. The distribution of complainants is shown in Table 1.

TABLE 1.
Sources of Reports Regarding Suspicion of Child Neglect/Abuse

Report From	Report To		
	Welfare	Police	Total
Anonymous	15	1	16
Hospital	14	1	15
Neighbour	9	6	15
Landlord/Boarding Mistress	2	10	12
Relative	8	3	11
School	7	0	7
Public Health Service	7	0	7
Psychiatrist	4	0	4
Priest	1	0	1
Baby-sitter	0	1	1
Self-Report	1	0	1
Total	68	21	89

Approximately 60 percent of these reports (including anonymous ones) originated with persons who had some kind of interpersonal but unofficial link with the individuals they reported. To date, no one has attempted to delineate an "informant syndrome"; but the ease with which households can be brought to the attention of authorities suggests that certain kinds of households are quite vulnerable once they come under official scrutiny.[8] Indeed, a fair proportion of suspected persons maintained that a "grudge" lay at the basis of the reports against them. However, once a household is reported, the child worker may perceive aspects of that household which to her mind are suspicious and require investigation quite apart from the content of the initial report. Here, of course, there is an important typification that is employed – that of the "typical informant." For official purposes the motivations of informants are those of concerned, responsible citizens, moved by a sense of civic duty. Consider, for example, the expression of neighbourhood concern in the anonymous letter reproduced below:

Dear Sirs or Madam:

Perhaps writing this letter will be all in vain but at least I'll know that you people know what is going on.

At [address] there is a family with at least eight children, these children are neglected by the parents who don't even care if the children ever eat or wash. The family in question is on the Relief, not because the father can't find work but because he and his wife are too busy getting drunk all day and night. The food which the Relief is supposed to supply is sold to buy liquor for the mother and father and their so called friends. If the neighbors on the [neighborhood] didn't feed these children they would starve. Not only do some of them give them food but clothing also. At six-thirty or seven o'clock these children are poked up on the attic of the house where they all sleep. The house is infested with mice and some say even rats. There is no water or sewerage in this house, the water is also supplied by the neighbors.

Two of the children are sick, one of them has a 'running ear' and is supposed to have gotten an x-ray three or four weeks ago, but the parents don't care enough to see that this is done.

The small children are kept in the house all the time and to look at them you would think they were in some tropical country running around without any clothing on. Sometimes they might have on a dress full of holes.

When family allowance day comes around, do they buy food or clothes for the children, they might buy a bit of food for themselves after they have their stock of liquor in for a few days. I don't know if there is any law about making home brew for one's use but that is one of their accomplishments also.

You might say that I'm making things sound worse than they really are, I'm not even making it sound half as bad as it really is. You have to see to believe.

When anything is cooked it's always done by an eleven year old girl and then it's always potatoes. The mother says she can't do it, her back is bad, so she lies on the couch getting her strength back for tonights spree.

All you have to do is look through their windows which they don't even bother to cover to see what goes on. Don't you think something should be done for these poor children, before it is too late. They aren't delinquents yet so why not give them a chance, take them from this misery in which they live and give them a good home, even if it is a foster one.

(SGD) Concerned

Whatever the motivation of the writer – and there is an indication of nosiness (looking through the window) and perhaps of a grudge (the reference to "so-called friends") – the District Office responded speedily, both to the suspicion of neglect and to the suspicion regarding the misuse of welfare assistance. In fact, the first official to arrive was the family's social-assistance officer.

Families who have received, or who are receiving, welfare assistance are particularly vulnerable to accusations of neglect/abuse. First, the Department will already have a dossier containing information about them and evaluations of them which aid officials in constructing biographies of these persons with greater assurance. Officials tend to have multiple sources of information about "multi-problem families"; one wonders whether such a gloss is in part a function of different official sources of information – a consequence of bureaucratic coordination through which different sets of officials contribute information about different aspects of the same family and then group them under a "multi-problem." Second, families receiving welfare assistance are afraid of attracting official scrutiny and of losing their assistance. Third, welfare clients apparently feel that officials disapprove of their modes of living. A recent national Canadian survey of such clients found that, "... 57% of the recipients with children think that the worker disapproves of the way they bring up their children" (Federal-Provincial Study Group on Alienation, 1974:31). Therefore there is a strong likelihood that many parents suspected of neglect/abuse will react with fear and hostility and that such reactions will tend to confirm the suspicions of the investigator. In two-thirds of the cases I examined, the parents either had received or were receiving welfare assistance; and less than 10 percent could be considered middle-class in terms of socio-economic resources.

Because welfare officers, including child workers, live with both their societal and organizational stocks of knowledge, the themes to which they attribute relevance, in the course of their investigations, are at times combinations of these different aspects of their life-worlds. For example, the following memo instructs the welfare officer to investigate an instance of suspected neglect: "I have today received a call from a gentleman who lives in the apartment beneath that of Mrs. X. He reports that Mrs. X has 3 children, aged 4, 5 and 7 and that these children are left alone at night, quite often until the wee-small hours of the morning. She is said to bring home men on occasions, and to have them in her apartment until 4 or 5 AM. It could be that the children are being neglected ... Maybe Mrs. X requires supervision." That the woman in question leaves her young children to fend for themselves during the night may well be organizational grounds for suspicion of neglect. That she brings men home to spend the night appears to be related to more general moral typifications, than to neglect as such. The official's linking of these two themes, which are not necessarily inter-connected, indicates the complexity of deciding not only what themes are relevant, but of what exactly the issue to be investigated consists.

Whether a household is reported by unofficial or official informants, it is selected through a variety of typifications, and hence for a variety of motives, the latter acting on the basis of medical and clinical constructs, and the former as dutiful citizens. The many subjective interpretations in a report are initially standardized by the report itself as a gloss of 'suspected neglect/abuse,' an official category that makes sense (as a report of suspi-

cion) to relevant officials. The officials then gain entry to a variety of
households for a multitude of reasons on the basis of the validity of the gloss
– as it is represented in a stock of knowledge that is meaningful to them.
Their subsequent evaluation of what they perceive is then a function of the
relevance of this stock of knowledge to what they see, and not necessarily
to whatever elements elicited the invocation of the gloss in the first place.

For administrative purposes each child-welfare worker is assigned an
area of the city and all cases of child welfare within it. Thus each child
worker handles a range of cases which include adoptions, foster homes,
unwed mothers, and "protection" (the official designation for neglect/
abuse cases which are handled by a separate division in the department).
Since protection cases are not equitably distributed in all areas of the city,
some child workers are required to handle many more such cases than are
others.[9] Protection cases are regarded as "dirty work" mainly because
they place the child worker in the untenable position of having to reconcile
major ideological contradictions about how such cases are perceived, not
only in order to reach a decision, but actually to handle the case itself. As
one worker put it: "You have to take one side or the other; otherwise you
get torn apart."

The contradictions the child worker is faced with include the following:
as a member of the wider life-world she/he is aware that many parents
sometimes strike their children without intending to injure them, in the
course of discipline, and that this sometimes occurs in a moment of anger.[10]
On the other hand, as a member of an organizational life-world, she is well
aware of publicity through the mass media, should serious harm befall
a child who had been brought to the attention of the child-welfare authorities,
but who had not been found neglected or abused. Hence the maxim,
"Better to err on the side of the safety of the child."

A second major contradiction revolves about the way child workers
perceive the sentiments of a typical parent toward his child. Child workers
are often parents themselves and experience the deep feelings of attachment parents can have for their children. Nevertheless, as a member of an
organizational life-world, one of the child workers' tasks is to remove
children from their parental homes, and to face the often hostile and
sometimes belligerent reactions of the parents involved. A consequence of
this contradiction is that child workers may perceive themselves as a
threat, thereby constructing a hypothetical reaction compatible with their
own self-perceptions (see Schutz and Luckmann, 1973:196). Although this
does not eliminate the conflict for child workers, it does make it intelligible
for them. One worker commented: "I'm trying to do home visits now, and
they're [the mothers] never home. Probably see me coming and don't
answer the door. I'd probably do the same thing in their position, you
know." Another worker responded: "My God, we're the biggest threat. I

can't understand workers who say those people are nuts because they behave that way [aggressively]. *Imagine* how a mother feels when we come to take her kids away.''

A third major contradiction is within the organizational life-world, specifically in the different stages of the development of a case. The child worker may be required to apprehend (the official term) a child, and then to initiate legal proceedings to have that child removed from the parental home for a longer period. After having performed these punitive tasks, the worker will be expected, at least formally, to engage in the counselling and ''rehabilitation'' of the parents. Workers who take the latter phase seriously find it difficult to switch roles before the same audience, while convincing that audience (the parents) that these roles are connected to one another in a logical and beneficial way.

That protection cases are regarded as ''dirty work'' is reflected in the official statements and unofficial policies of the Department of Social Services. The annual reports make fleeting references to protection cases, stating only that they fall within the purview of the department. No statistical breakdown of processed cases is offered. In comparison, the processing and disposition of adoption cases are described in great detail. But adoption cases are regarded by the department and its workers as happy events. As well, the procedures for handling adoption cases are outlined extensively in the regulations of the department. By contrast, only cursory guidelines exist for dealing with suspected neglect, and many of these are only simple re-statements of the Articles of the Child Welfare Act. Unofficially, workers are encouraged to work on their adoption cases, and the number of adoptions successfully carried out is regarded as a major criterion of the department's expertise.

The worker who turns to the regulations for assistance in evaluating an instance of suspected neglect/abuse will discover the following statement: ''Every Welfare Officer, at some time in his career, will have brought to his attention a child who is not receiving the care and upbringing considered necessary for his proper development. This child, for some reason, or for a number of reasons, may be considered a neglected child. Every such complaint or report of neglect must be investigated to determine its authenticity and the extent of the neglect'' (Section 221). This is the only guideline suggesting what the worker should search for in interpreting an instance of suspicion. The remainder of the regulations go on to describe procedures (apprehension, courtroom procedures, types of wardship that can be requested) applicable only after the worker has decided that she is dealing with a case of neglect/abuse. Thus we return to the problem as initially stated: how does the worker get from suspicion to decision?

The Child Welfare Act, 1972, provides twenty criteria under which a child (under the age of sixteen) can be considered neglected. These criteria are summations that imply that the welfare officer already has arrived at a decision which can be glossed in a manner compatible with these legal glosses. Thus the most commonly used subsection for the apprehension of a child (Article 2, Subsection [p] [iv]) states that a neglected child is one "... whose parents, or surviving parent, or guardian or other person in whose charge he may be, cannot by reason of misfortune, disease or infirmity properly care for him, or are unfit to have charge of him, or refuse to maintain him." The question of how to understand, for example, "misfortune" and "are unfit to have charge of him" is left to the welfare officer.

When a welfare officer decides that there are "... reasonable or probable grounds for believing that a child is a neglected child ..." (*op. cit.*), the child can be apprehended without a warrant and kept in care for ten days without a court hearing. If legal proceedings are initiated by the welfare officer, there are four possible decision categories: (1) the judge can throw out the case; (2) the judge can decide that the child should remain within the household, but that the family should be subject to the supervision of the Department of Social Services through the visits of the child worker; (3) the child should be made a "temporary ward" of the Director of Social Services for an initial period of twelve months and be placed in a foster home or an institution; (4) the child should be made a "permanent ward" of the Director of Social Services. In this case the child is taken from the household for an indefinite period, and under certain circumstances, may become available for adoption.[11]

At the outset of this essay I suggested that the application of rule-to-case by the invocation of "special knowledge" was a problematic accomplishment for members of bureaucratic organizations, in the sense that such work proceeded through a process of interpretation on the part of officials, which was itself screened through largely uncodified bureaucratic, professional, and other common-sense typifications.

I then delineated the development of the battered-child syndrome as one kind of typification that has become available to child-welfare workers. This construct is based on certain assumptions which translate the instance into a cause-and-effect relationship between motivation and behaviour. Application of elements of the syndrome to elements of the instance does not solve the problem of interpretation, however, since the investigator still must proceed according to the principle of compatibility, suggested by Schutz and Luckmann. Presumably there are other kinds of bureaucratic and more general common-sense assumptions underlying the principle of compatibility that render constructs such as the syndrome relevant to the elements of the instance.

Neither in the way that the reporting of suspicion is done, nor in the codified knowledge available to the child worker, is the problematic nature of bureaucratic interpretation solved. One may suggest that the nature of reporting, the availability of constructs such as the syndrome, and formal guidelines do provide significant resources for the child worker; but that they are not sufficient conditions for the satisfactory bureaucratic elucidation of the instance.

The extended-case method cannot clarify the full range of common-sense assumptions behind the processing of instances of suspicion; nor can this approach claim to validate the identification of such assumptions. But by adopting a sequential perspective to the accretion of information through time, it can attempt to identify how officials react to 'new' information, and whether they alter their interpretations to account for what happened. Given that officials apparently do alter their perceptions in their quest for an intelligible, explanatory story-line, one can then suggest the kinds of assumptions upon which such changes are based, and thereby further the process of delineating the nature of bureaucratic interpretation.

Our case is presented as a series of nine events and one interlude as it developed over a period of two weeks. During this time a decision was taken, judicial proceedings were completed, and a disposition was accomplished. The viewpoint is largely that of the child worker in charge of the investigation as she assimilates information, and the viewpoints of others who try to make sense of what happened. That she is never satisfied about arriving at the truth of the instance does not affect the disposition of the case, since it proceeds to its completion within a life-world of administrative imperatives.

Each event is followed by a commentary. Taken together, the commentaries should be read as an analysis of the case.

Event I: The Priest's Tale, Friday, September 20.
On Friday afternoon the child-welfare supervisor received a telephone call from a parish priest, who was well known to the Department of Social Services, reporting that a member of the Worth family, either the father, Abe Sr., or his son, Abe Jr., was leading his niece "astray." He did not know her name, referred to her as "the niece," and thought she was fourteen years of age. He heard that the niece had left the Worth household and had gone to stay with another aunt, but that Abe Sr. had "forcibly" removed her from this household and returned her to the Worths. The priest added that one of the Abes plied the niece with "drink and smokes," and that the niece's father had been "murdered" at some time in the past.

The child-welfare worker in charge of this area was dispatched to investigate the Worth household. On her arrival she found the house empty, except for a fourteen-year-old, who told her that all the others were out in the family car. The worker discovered that the name of the niece was Diane. By that time it was after 5 PM on a Friday afternoon, and so the worker returned to the office; nothing could be done until Monday. At the office, she learned that Mr. Worth was receiving long-term social assistance. Long-term assistance, as distinct from short-term assistance, is allocated to heads of households who are certified, on medical grounds, to be unable to work indefinitely. Instead of visiting the welfare office once a month to collect their checks and to have their eligibility for assistance reviewed as do short-term assistance clients, long-term clients receive their checks by mail and have their eligibility reviewed once a year. According to the information supplied by the Worth's long-term-assistance caseworker, Mr. Worth was not employed, and could be considered unemployable. In addition, the Worths had a reputation for ''confrontation'' and for ''sticking together.''

Commentary: First Assumptions – Meaningful Relation and Biographical Stretch

The elements of this opening event concern (a) information received from persons (priest, social-assistance worker) who are considered to be authoritative in the organizational life-world of the welfare office; (b) intimations of violence associated with the household; and (c) reflections on the character of the household.

A significant assumption underlying these elements for the caseworker is that they are all related. Therefore they are not discrete items existing in association only because of the nature of the caseworker's investigative stance. Instead, because they have come together as a result of this mode of inquiry, some kind of meaningful relationship should exist among them. Furthermore, this relationship represents an objective reality that should exist apart from the sources and mode of inquiry of the investigator. An objective viewpoint is crucial if she is to explain her interpretation according to the relevancies of the organizational life-world. In this sense, a typification of the instance as ''suspicious'' is a paradigm of assumptions that generates social action; that is, it is problem-oriented, and it permits the caseworker to take decisions about what she perceives as problematic.

The assumption of ''meaningful relation'' in this instance is intimately connected to another assumption about sources of information. I suggested earlier that all reports are initially standardized under the gloss, ''suspected neglect/abuse''. But reports from persons of authority, or from official sources, are marked by a further characteristic: for bureaucratic purposes they are considered more accurate; the reporters are assumed to know whereof they speak; and they are assumed to be acting from objective motives of concern. Therefore the assumption of ''belief in authoritative sources'' overrides much of the skepticism of the caseworker in investigating an instance. Which informants are considered authoritative is related to bureaucratic conceptions of persons who are objectively motivated by concern for the public good.

The information provided by the parish priest associates an idea of force or violence with members of the Worth household. Moreover, the priest provides information that expands the relevance of the instance to illumi-nate the past history of relationships within the household. The assumption of 'biographical stretch' suggests that an instance is not an historical isolate, but that it is tied into a more comprehensive biographical picture, of which the instance is representative. In other words, the instance is placed in a wider context of relevance within which its idiosyncratic aspects are demonstrated to be integral to a more general pattern of behaviour in the household. Therefore it is understood as the way the persons concerned "usually" behave. That Diane is plied with alcohol and tobacco is informa-tion that begins to establish the biographical stretch of the household. As well, the information about the household's reputation for confrontation suggests that the family will be difficult to deal with.

Given the three assumptions suggested above, the caseworker considers the household, and its treatment of Diane, suspect. According to the typification of suspicion she takes a decision: to investigate the household. Since she is unable to pursue this until Monday, her sense of apprehension is maintained, while the "thematic relevance" of the instance for her bureaucratic task has been established (see Schutz and Luckmann, *op.cit.*:186ff.). But her interpretations of the relevance of the gloss of suspicion is hypothetical, in the sense suggested by Schutz and Luckmann (p. 196): "Our action is frequently adjusted so as to give rise to situations in which it is possible to determine whether a hypothetical relevance should be converted into a 'valid' relevance or be considered as void. If such confirmations or annulments are independent of our action, one must often simply 'wait'." Nevertheless, the probability of the translation of hypo-thetical relevance to valid relevance is high in this phase, since whatever information has been collected is internally consistent: it exhibits no major contradictions in perceived meaning.

Event II: In the Hospital, Saturday, September 21.
(a) *The Hospital Social Worker's Account*: In the early afternoon, Jennifer Worth, aged thirteen, was brought to the emergency department of the hospital by her sister, Betty, aged nineteen, and Betty's husband. Jennifer said that her father had beaten her (because her room had been untidy) about the face with his fists and then struck her on the head with a high-heeled shoe. When her scalp started to bleed he applied turpentine. He continued to beat her, and struck her on the left arm with his belt. Jennifer fled to Betty's house, four doors away, and Betty then brought her to the hospital.

The hospital social worker did not question Jennifer about the alleged beating, but Jennifer "offered" to show her the "strap mark" on her left arm. The social worker accepted the fact that a beating had taken place, and that a strap was used. The worker then spoke with Betty, whom she found "anxious" to discuss the incident. Betty said that about noon,

Diane, a cousin, and some of the younger Worth children had run to her home to report that their father was beating Jennifer, that Jennifer's head was cut, and that she was covered with blood. Betty telephoned the police and requested that a constable intervene. The police replied that as this was a family matter, that they could do nothing, and suggested that the matter be taken to Family Court on Monday. According to Betty, about one hour later Jennifer "escaped" to her home. Betty also said that she had not seen her father that morning, but that his car was parked in front of his door and that he never left home without it.

Betty added that there was a "lot of trouble" in the Worth home, and that her father occasionally had forced her mother to forge checks. He had done so the previous Sunday. Then he, Mrs. Worth, Betty, and her husband all went to a local pub and cashed the check. Betty had convinced her mother to leave Mr. Worth; she did so but Mr. Worth found where she was staying and convinced her to return home.

In her report the hospital social-worker wrote: "Betty provided this background in order to demonstrate why her mother would now go out of her way to protect her husband from any charge." She also noted that while there was "no love lost" between Betty and her father, Abe Worth, she did "not appear vindictive" in recounting the incidents.

Commentary: The Character of Informants

In interpreting the information received from Jennifer, her account of the beating, her physical appearance, and the motive she ascribes to her father, all appear to the social worker to co-exist in meaningful relation to one another. Betty's account places her father at home when the beating occurred. Her information about the relationship between Mr. and Mrs. Worth enables the social worker to stretch the biography of the household further: a multi-problem household containing instances of check-forging, and a wife leaving her husband.

The assumption of belief in authoritative sources, however, is not relevant since the informants are not officials. Unlike those of officials, the character and motivation of such persons is perceived as indeterminate. Therefore their motivation must be evaluated in order that sense be made of their information. The social worker takes pains to establish that although Betty does not like her father, she does not appear vindictive. Also, it is apparent that Betty is concerned for Jennifer since she brought her to the hospital, and since she willingly supplied the social worker with information. Because of these two pieces of evidence, Betty's motivation is interpreted as that of a good sibling, and her story as objective: she has no reason to lie about what really happened. Therefore the interpretation of the social worker is that Mr. Worth beat Jennifer.

(b) *Mrs. Worth's Account*: That afternoon the hospital social-worker telephoned Mrs. Worth to inform her that Jennifer was in the hospital. Mrs. Worth denied that her husband had beaten Jennifer. She then came to the hospital alone. By this time the child-welfare worker who had begun to investigate the Worths with reference to Diane had also been notified. When she arrived at the hospital, Mrs. Worth was already present, and she realized then that her two cases converged within a single household.

In the hospital, faced with two doctors, the social worker, and the child-welfare worker, Mrs. Worth did not deny the accounts of Jennifer and Betty but stated: "I don't know what was going on. I was in the other room. I'd never do that to one of my children."

Commentary: Further Assumptions – Contradiction and Official Definition
The problem of establishing what really happened is complicated by Mrs. Worth's denial that her husband beat Jennifer. Since the official definition of reality requires that the coincidence of an injured child and the accounts that purport to explain the child's condition be associated in a cause-and-effect relationship (in terms of someone doing something to that child), then contradictions in accounts cannot be treated as different perspectives of the same occasion. Instead, the official perspective of the reality of the instance must assume that contradictions in accounts indicate that someone is lying. Then the task of the official is to establish who is telling the truth. Lying or truthfulness are predicated upon the motivations (once again) of the persons involved to fabricate, and inferences about their reasons for doing so will establish whether or not they do so.

In this instance Betty had provided a motive as to why her mother would protect her father. Mrs. Worth's account to the authorities at the hospital throws doubt on her initial story over the telephone. Not only does she change her version when faced with authority but she also appears defensive, as if suspicion might also fall on her ("I'd never do that to one of my children"). Bittner (1973:115), among others, has pointed out that: "All 'accounts' ... are unavoidably and irremediably tied to the social settings that occasion them or within which they are situated ... the tie of accounts to settings is unavoidable and irremediable because the accounts derive their sensibility and warrant from it." The definition of social setting that officials consider relevant is one that is compatible with their perceptions of their own tasks. Thus they tend to interpret accounts offered in the setting in terms of their own "motivational relevance" (see Schutz and Luckmann, *op. cit.*:208ff.). Their own motivations in investigating the instances are not punitive, at least for organizational purposes, but instead are beneficial ones aimed at helping the household concerned. Therefore they expect the object of investigation to accept and to react in a manner consistent with this positive definition of setting. Thus Mrs. Worth was not supposed to feel threatened, and her change in story indicated evasiveness rather than intimidation, as did her defensiveness.

At this point the hypothetical typification of the instance as suspected abuse remains consistent with previous interpretations: Mrs. Worth is probably lying; Jennifer and Betty are probably telling the truth; and Mr.

Worth's character remains consistent with the incident of the previous day concerning Diane.

(c) *The Medical Examination*: The doctor described Jennifer's condition as pale, frightened, thin, dirty, and undernourished-looking; when questioned she became upset, and spoke incoherently at first; throughout she sobbed intermittently; she was unable to sit up without feeling faint and she collapsed several times.

The head wound itself was described as a ''2-centimetre-long superficial bleeding laceration on the back of her head.'' (It was closed with a single suture.) Adjacent to the wound there was evidence of an old scar. The right side of her face was swollen with bruising; and there was swelling and bruising about her left eye, bruising on the neck and upper chest, and small lacerations down the right side of her face, as well as assorted small bruises on her limbs. She had a large red weal across her left upper arm which the doctor reported as ''apparently from a belt blow.'' The doctor's summary of the examination was stated as: (a) ''multiple soft tissue injuries,'' (b) ''psychological trauma,'' and (c) ''malnutrition and failure to thrive.'' Jennifer told the doctor that there were other young children in the household who were beaten by her father.

Commentary: The Connectedness of Assumptions

The doctor's investigation is crucial to establishing the typification of neglect/abuse. Although he refrains from stating outright that Jennifer had been beaten, he does typify her injuries, her emotional state, and her nutritional state according to elements of the neglected/battered-child syndrome; that is, according to the assumption of ''meaningful relation,'' he presents aspects of the child's condition as if they were connected in a causal way. It is this connectedness that permits a comparison with the syndrome.

Of particular significance for the interpretation of the instance by officials is that the doctor is prepared to bring into association statements about physical condition and the behavioural reactions of the child. Evidence of previous injury (a scar on the head), numerous bruises on the face, chest, and limbs, and lacerations on the face, along with evidence of malnutrition, are all consistent with elements of the neglected/battered-child syndrome. But, by themselves, these symptoms cannot easily be judged out of the ordinary for a child in a large family, where an accumulation of physical contacts between family members may not be unusual. However, the behavioural symptoms described as ''psychological trauma'' accompanying the physical symptoms are judged to be unusual and provide an explication of the instance, since the latter is assumed to be a *result* of the former. In this sense, a measure of the child's injury is her reaction to whatever happened to her. But, according to the official definition of the hospital setting, she should not react as she does unless something really did happen to her.

The kind of person who evoked such behavioural reactions in the girl is still open to question. But parents are more vulnerable to being cast in the role of causal agent than are siblings. By the age of thirteen, the oedipal and electra complexes are expected to have run their active courses, whereas sibling rivalry may still be relevant and therefore not unusual. Thus injuries caused by normal conflicts between siblings should not evoke such behavioural reactions, whereas the unusual expression of conflicts between parents and child may do so.

Earlier I suggested that for officials, an account is indicative of official perceptions of the setting. In this instance the assumption of *meaningful relation* connecting the gloss of psychological trauma to that of multiple soft-tissue injuries means that the behaviours constituting the gloss antedate the child's presence in the hospital setting. Therefore it is not the hospital setting that evokes trauma in Jennifer, and for official purposes, her being frightened is not related to the modes of interrogation of the investigator.

The assumptions of meaningful relation and official definition of the setting, made relevant in the medical examination, are strengthened by Jennifer's contribution to the relevance of the assumption of *biographical stretch* in understanding the household. She maintains that other siblings are beaten by her father. Therefore what happened to her was not an idiosyncratic instance, but a common-place one that widens the relevance of a typification of abuse which officials are constructing.

(d) *The Apprehension*: When Mrs. Worth came to the hospital she was informed that Jennifer had been apprehended under Article 2 (p) (xiv) of the Child Welfare Act, which reads: " 'neglected child' means a child who is unlawfully assaulted, ill-used or treated with cruelty or neglect by his parents or guardian." The official typification of the instance clearly appeared to be one of child abuse. Jennifer's story was accepted fully. Mrs. Worth's disclaimer over the telephone was discounted as being consistent with the neglected/battered-child syndrome wherein parents protect one another. Mrs. Worth's wavering in the hospital was interpreted as evidence that she was indeed covering up for her husband, a motive which had been supplied by Betty.

The official acceptance of Jennifer's and Betty's stories is indicated further by the choice of the article of apprehension: Article 2 (p) (xiv) specifies the *active abuse* of the child by parents. Child-welfare workers usually choose Article 2 (p) (iv) as grounds for apprehension because it is more diffuse, and because it relies more on emphasizing the *passive neglect* of the child.

After being informed of the apprehension, Mrs. Worth said that after many years of unemployment, Mr. Worth had a chance for a job; she wondered if the apprehension would affect this. The hospital social-worker encouraged Mrs. Worth to do everything possible to get him to work. But to

the child-welfare worker, Mrs. Worth appeared nervous about returning to her husband with the news of the apprehension. She asked Mrs. Worth if her husband "would take it out on her." Mrs. Worth laughed faintly and replied: "Oh no. There's lots of woods around our house for me to get to."
Commentary: The Reach for Consistency
The officials involved in typifying the instances have already decided that Mr. Worth is a violent person who has beaten Jennifer and perhaps others of his children. They have also decided, in accordance with the battered-child syndrome and the information supplied by Betty, that Mrs. Worth would protect her husband. When Mrs. Worth expresses worry that the apprehension may affect her husband's chance of employment, the caseworker perceives this as an attempt to gain sympathy for Mr. Worth, and as an attempt to articulate her fear of her husband. In accordance with the assumptions of meaningful relation and biographical stretch, if Mr. Worth is a violent man, then Mrs. Worth must be frightened of his reaction. When the worker asks Mrs. Worth whether she is frightened, she receives a reply which confirms her suspicion and she concludes that Mrs. Worth is "terrified" of her husband. According to the way in which the instance has been interpreted and the case constructed, the perceived expression *of* fear is indicative of the reason *to* fear.

That Mrs. Worth's response could be given a different interpretation is considered irrelevant at this stage, since the interpretation of the elements of the case exhibits a high degree of internal consistency and compatibility: the behaviours of Jennifer, Betty, and Mrs. Worth, as well as their compatibility with the interpretation of 'what really happened.' The negative evaluation of Mr. Worth's character is also consistent and unanimous; hence the assurance with which Article 2 (p) (xiv) is invoked as grounds for the apprehension.

Therefore another assumption which appears to underlie the construction of a story-line by officials is their tendency to reach for consistency in interpreting their evidence. This assumption is a corollary of the previously cited assumption that contradiction in accounts is indicative of lying. An unproblematic case, therefore, is one which can be interpreted with a high degree of internal consistency, and one in which the constructed cause-and-effect relationship of 'what really happened' and 'why' can be intelligibly represented to other relevant officials.

Event III: In the Office, Monday, September 23
During this day various items of information were brought to the attention of officials by persons whom they considered to be "authoritative sources":
1. The hospital social-worker telephoned the child-welfare supervisor to reiterate that Jennifer was terrified of her father.
2. Later the principal of the school attended by a number of the Worth

children telephoned to say that none of the Worth children had appeared in school that day. He added that some of the pupils were talking of a knifing that involved the Worths, of Abe Jr.'s being Diane's boyfriend, and of his being a bad influence on her.

3. The Worths' long-term assistance worker said that he was convinced of Mr. Worth's being a "very heavy drinker."
4. The matter of the check forgeries was raised with Mrs. Worth over the telephone. She admitted that they had occurred, but maintained that the person who had been bilked would be reimbursed.
5. The supervisor, who had not seen Jennifer, described the scalp laceration as "a great bloody hole in her head." Fearing violence, she instructed the caseworker not to visit the Worth home by herself, but to be accompanied by another welfare officer. The supervisor and caseworker discussed the case and concluded "that we had a hornets' nest on our hands." They decided that it was too dangerous to leave Diane in the Worth home and that she too should be apprehended.
6. The school principal called again to say he had heard that Kent Worth, aged twelve, had a "burn" on his shoulder.

Commentary: The Halo Effect of Interpretation
The official interpretation of these elements is that they support the negative evaluation of Mr. Worth's character. Furthermore, another member of the household (Abe Jr.) also appears to be associated with violence; we hear once again that Abe Jr. appears to be corrupting Diane, supporting the parish priest's information.

The halo effect of interpretation that is generated by assumptions of meaningful relation and biographical stretch is nicely illustrated by the supervisor's rendering of the two-centimeter superficial laceration as "a great bloody hole in her head." The supervisor and caseworker interpret the household to be a dangerous setting for children. Therefore they decide that Diane should be removed, and that the condition of the other six Worth children living in the household should be evaluated. The supervisor also cautions the caseworker to take along a male welfare officer when she visits the household. This is routine office procedure when there is fear that violence may be directed towards the caseworker.

Interlude: Is What Happened Then Happening Now? Tuesday, Sept. 24
The caseworker obtained the social-assistance and child-welfare files that had been compiled on the Worths. The household was found to contain the following persons:

Abe Sr.	born	1929	Kent	"	1962
Mrs. Worth	"	1933	Ron	"	1964
Abe Jr.	"	1959	Martha	"	1965
Lucy	"	1960	Lorrie	"	1966
Jennifer	"	1961	Diane (niece)	"	1960

In addition, the eldest daughters, Mary (born 1954), and Betty (born 1955), had married and established their own households. The Worths had married in 1953. Mr. Worth had no formal education and had worked as a labourer until 1967, when he began to receive long-term social assistance because he suffered from a hiatus hernia. His father had spent many years in a mental hospital; three of his brothers also received social assistance, and the fourth was presumed to have committed suicide. In the early 1960s a welfare officer described Mr. Worth in the following way:

> He is uncooperative and difficult to reason with. He does not seem to have a great deal of concern for his family. He hasn't made much effort to support them over the years or to give his children the guidance, discipline and affection they needed. Unable to face his shortcomings, he tries to blame all his failures on his ill health and thinks that the Welfare 'owes him a living.' ... On the whole Mr. Worth seems to be a cowardly, lazy man, who's main concern is for his own Welfare. It is doubtful if any amount of counselling could change his attitudes, and I doubt that he could ever give his children a decent home and upbringing.''

At that time the family was living in a small cabin, without electricity, tables, or chairs. The whole family slept in two beds. Mr. Worth had on occasion experienced the pressure of the Department of Social Assistance. In 1970 he refused to undergo corrective surgery for his hiatus hernia. This provoked the regional administrator to write the following memo, which reads in part: "Mr. Worth has the right to refuse surgery but when a recipient of assistance will not undergo medical treatment to correct his complaint, then the Department has the right to suspend LTA [Long-Term Assistance]. Mr. Worth should be told in no uncertain terms that if he refuses surgery to correct his hernia, then LTA will be suspended ... [His refusal] is tantamount to his refusing rehabilitation measures which could facilitate his return to the labour market.'' Although Mr. Worth continued to refuse to undergo surgery, his assistance was not suspended, for a reason which will become relevant in the conclusion to this essay.

From the files it was also learned that the Worths had been reported for suspected child-neglect in 1964 and 1965. In April 1966 the department considered requesting temporary wardship for the children, but the welfare officer in charge felt that this would be difficult to obtain; as she wrote then, "Again both Mr. and Mrs. Worth express a deep love for their children and would fight to retain custody of them. Consequently anything short of demonstrable neglect would not suffice to convince the court. It was felt that if the children could have been taken for awhile, it might shock the parents into taking a greater interest in keeping both the children and the house clean.'' Consequently, child welfare was geared to apprehend the children in order to teach their parents a lesson about cleanliness; and the welfare officer awaited a pretext which would make such an action intelligible to the court. Such an occasion occurred in December, 1966.

One night shortly after midnight, a neighbour called to say that Betty had appeared on her doorstep after being beaten by her father, and that she was afraid to return home. The child-welfare worker, whose evaluations of the household were cited previously, arrived with two constables. Mr. Worth denied beating Betty. Betty herself was found to have numerous cuts, scrapes, and bruises on her face, arms, and legs, and a large gash on the back of her head. Betty said her father had gone to see her mother in the hospital that morning, and that he had told her to stay at home. Instead she ran errands for the neighbours to earn a few cents. When he returned, Abe Jr. told him what Betty had done. According to Betty, Mr. Worth then slapped her, struck her, kicked her, and knocked her down. As she fell her head struck the corner of the day bed, opening the gash in her scalp.

In her account of the situation in the home, the child worker stressed that she found conditions of "unnecessary and willful neglect." The inventory of elements that she attributed to this condition included the following: seven children were sleeping in two beds, and "in one bed five children and a cat huddled together for warmth"; the children were filthy, dressed in filthy rags, and covered with filthy ragged blankets, while Mr. Worth slept by himself on a day bed in the kitchen (the warmest room) and was covered with six warm wool blankets; whereas the children had no decent clothing, Mr. Worth had a suit, a few white shirts, neckties, and three sets of long underwear. In addition, the floor of the house was so dirty "it was sticky to walk upon"; and there was little food in the house – one quarter of a loaf of bread, a tin of molasses, and tea.

That night all the children were apprehended. A few days later Mr. Worth was arrested on a charge of assault. The evidence was provided by the doctor who had examined Betty, by Betty herself, and by her older sister, Mary. Mr. Worth was convicted and sentenced to a fine of fifty dollars or thirty days in prison. His fine was paid by his brother, a welfare recipient, an act which outraged the welfare officer.

Shortly afterwards the Worth home burned down, and all eight children were made temporary wards for one year and placed in foster homes. With financial aid from the department, the Worths began to rebuild their home. The department maintained that the children could return to their parents only when they had a "decent" home, and when the latter showed a "considerable change in their attitudes and values."

By March 1967, less than three months after Mary and Betty were placed in foster homes, the Child Welfare Division recommended that they be returned to their parents because they caused too much trouble to their foster parents and because they wanted to go home. Mary, Betty, and the other older children were caught lying, stealing, placing false fire alarms, and running back to their parents. When Mary, then thirteen, was placed in a foster home she appeared to be afraid of her father, and said that she had no wish to return home. She was described as slovenly, sly, dishonest, and her behaviour was marked by foul language and dirty habits. Betty, then twelve, was termed brazen and rather wild. She also expressed a desire not to see her father again. Her behaviour in the foster home was similar to Mary's.

In March 1967, the child worker commented, "they are intolerable and will have to be removed immediately," and recommended that the girls either be sent to a reform school or returned to their parents. Hence, three months after the girls had become temporary wards, they were returned to their parents, and two months later, all the children were back at the Worths. The rationale for this swift about-face by the authorities was the Worths' re-building of their home: this work was interpreted as indicative of a major change in the attitudes and values of the parents.

Commentary: Temporal Triangulation

A corollary of the assumption of biographical stretch is the temporal triangulation of present, past, and future. This assumption can be read as follows: if a state of affairs is perceived as being true in the present, it was probably also true in the past, and is likely to be true in the future. If the relevant 'truth' of the past is demonstrated to be compatible with an analogous 'truth' in the present, then the relevant reality of both past and present are strengthened; and one truth may be perceived as a continuation of the other. Since officials have available only a limited number of such triangulation points, they must infer that compatibility between analogous elements can be read as a meaningful relation that fills in the information gap between tenses. When present and past are shown to be compatible, they simplify the triangulation of what may be expected in the future. Such a temporal triangulation forms an important resource in the interpretation of instances, where the disposition of a case depends not only on 'what really happened,' but also on 'what is likely to happen' in the future if no intervention takes place.

The welfare records of the Worths, as "contractual accounts" (Garfinkel, 1967:198ff), are instructive for the caseworker. These records provide elements which are congruent with the case, as it is being developed in the present. For example, the Worths have a history of child neglect/abuse. The current caseworker appreciates the difficulties the previous worker had in making a case against the Worths prior to the incident leading to the apprehension. An axiom in the department is that "dirt is not enough" to convince a judge to grant wardship. Mr. Worth's moral character in the present appears consistent with the descriptions recorded in 1966, and he is a convicted child-abuser. The judge found him guilty of assaulting Betty. One can assume, from the reports of the children's behaviour in their foster homes in 1967, that the Worth home environment exerted a destructive influence on their moral character. Furthermore, Betty's age at the time she was injured in 1966, and the nature of the injuries she suffered, appear to be strikingly similar to those of Jennifer.

In triangulating the past with the present, there appears to be a consistent pattern of harmful behaviour toward their children within the personae and characters of the heads of the Worth household. Since the past confirms the present, this strengthens the evaluation of the caseworker that nothing has changed – the typified biography of the family has remained unaltered through time.

Moreover, the sequential entry of the case record into the construction of the case in 1974 occurs when a decision regarding Jennifer has already been reached, a decision based on an overwhelming consistency in the interpretation of information collected. Thus, although the information of the case record can be read hypothetically in various ways, in this instance it is read as supporting the decision of apprehension that has already been taken. The justification of Jennifer's apprehension – to protect *her* – is fully apparent when officials read the triangulation of present and past as a gloss on what the future would likely hold for Jennifer, were she not apprehended. Of course, it also intensified the worries of the officials regarding Diane.

Event IV: In the Worth Home, Wednesday, September 25
In the morning the caseworker, accompanied by the Worth's long-term assistance worker, made her first visit to the Worth home. Mr. Worth was not there, but his car was.

The caseworker's first concern was for the Worth niece, Diane, who was still in the household. Mrs. Worth said that Diane's father had not been murdered (as the parish priest had reported), but that he had burned to death in a house fire. She then described in detail how "bad" and uncaring was Diane's mother; and how she and "others" drank their way through each week. Mrs. Worth emphasized that no incident whatsoever had occurred that would have forcibly removed Diane from the home of a relative.

The caseworker took Diane to the car where they spoke in privacy. Diane said that she preferred to live at the Worths because Mrs. Worth did not drink, and Mr. Worth did so rarely. When asked whether she herself drank she replied that she did not, but that she did smoke the odd cigarette for "fun." She added that she was not Abe Jr.'s girlfriend, but that the Worth family did tease her as if she were. She admitted to missing school often because she did not enjoy it, but added that Mr. Worth made her attend school, because otherwise he would "get into trouble with the welfare."

The caseworker asked her about the previous Friday's incident. Diane replied that instead of going to school that morning, she had stopped off at her mother's brother's home, where the people present began to drink heavily. (She added that her uncle once introduced her to beer, which made her feel ill.) Frightened, she went into the bedroom. When Mr. Worth arrived to collect her, she was ashamed to leave the bedroom immediately because she would have to admit to missing school again. But she did come out within a few minutes and left with Mr. Worth and Abe Jr. She insisted that no force or coercion had been used on her; on the contrary, Mr. Worth had "saved" her. She then said that she would swear to this story in court.

The caseworker and Diane re-entered the house. Here Mrs. Worth denied that her husband had caused all of Jennifer's injuries, and was supported in this by Abe Jr., aged sixteen; by Kent, aged twelve; and by Diane herself. Furthermore, Kent supplied a second version of the Saturday incident. The children had been building a shack in the yard, and Jennifer had knocked down part of it on purpose. Angered, Kent struck Jennifer over the head with a piece of clapboard, opening her scalp. He said he had no knowledge of his father striking Jennifer afterwards, since he then watched television. Abe Jr. and Diane supported his story of how Jennifer received her scalp laceration.

Mrs. Worth then attacked Betty, calling her a "liar" and volunteering the fact that twice she had attempted to commit suicide. She could not understand why Betty had lied in the hospital on Saturday after all her parents had done for her. She added that Betty herself was an unfit mother. She and her husband had seen Betty tie her baby's arms and legs when the child was one month old in order to change its diapers. The cords had left bruises on the baby's limbs.

Commentary: Retrospective Interpretation

Her visit to the Worth home brought to the caseworker's attention discrepancies in the story-line she and others were constructing. She had gone there with a hypothetical construction of the case as one of child abuse, on the basis of which a decision had been taken to apprehend Jennifer. In other words, the contours of the constructed case had begun to be routinized; and so too were her expectations about the explication of elements that had been made relevant. The information that she expected to collect should have been compatible and consistent with that already interpreted.

Schutz and Luckmann (*op.cit.*:187), among others, have pointed out that: "... the unfamiliar draws attention to itself within the surroundings of the familiar." They note further that new themes are imposed upon our perceptions when there is "... an enforced change of theme, which happens as a result of a break in automatic expectations" (p. 189). Then we must consider the hypothetical relevance of these new elements for interpretations that are already deemed relevant to the problem. Finally, "... if one cannot be routinely oriented in a situation, one must explicate it" (p. 191).

Contradictions and discrepancies in meaningful relations and in biographical stretch highlight new elements, or old ones that need to be re-interpreted, if the internal consistency and intelligibility of the story-line is to be maintained. Therefore a corollary of the assumption that perceived contradictions indicate untruthfulness is that discrepancy casts doubts.

The first discrepancy perceived by the caseworker is that Mr. Worth's car is home but he is not. One method of resolving discrepancy is through the assumption of retrospective interpretation, whereby the hypothetical relevance of experience for the interpretation of the temporal present is affected by the way in which the past is perceived (see Schutz and Luckmann, *op. cit.*:196). New information perceived in the present affects the way elements were evaluated in the past, thereby affecting the way these elements, or their analogous continuations, are interpreted in the present, and projected into the future.

The perceived meaning of the present is inextricably related to the perceived meaning of the past; but the meaning given to the past is dependent on the interpretation of the present, thus affecting what is expected in the future. Therefore, "... what the situation on any particular occasion is understood to have been may be revised subsequently in the light of later events. Consequently, what the situation 'really was' and what the actors 'really did' on a particular occasion are continually open to re-definition" (Wilson, 1970:701). In this way a constructed story-line continually adapts to changes in its environment to preserve its internal consistency and intelligibility to relevant audiences.

According to the welfare files on the Worths, in 1966 Mrs. Worth stated that Betty lied all the time. In 1967, according to the evaluation of Betty in the foster home, she was "brazen" and she told "lies." Betty placed Mr. Worth at the scene of the injury because of the presence of his car outside his home. She stated that he never left home without his car. But during this visit the car is present and Mr. Worth is not. Betty may have been mistaken, or she may have lied; in any case her association may not have been valid. Mr. Worth may not have been home at the time Jennifer received the scalp laceration.

In her talk with Diane the caseworker perceived a number of discrepancies. Her father had not been murdered (*contra* the priest's tale). Mr. Worth hardly drinks (*contra* the long-term assistance worker's account). Diane herself says she does not drink (*contra* the accounts of the priest and the principal). Abe Jr. is not her boy friend and Mr. Worth encourages her to go to school (*contra* the principal's account). Most significant is the fact that there was no incident on Friday past; to the contrary, Mr. Worth rescued her (*contra* the priest's tale).

I mentioned earlier that officials assume a belief in authoritative sources of information. A corollary of this assumption is that such persons have no motivation to lie deliberately in their official capacities. But people do feel motivated to lie deliberately because they have matters to hide. The caseworker perceives no motive for Diane's lying about what happened on Friday. Other items of information then become relevant in retrospect. Apparently the social assistance worker who dealt with Diane's parents had said once that the Worth home was "paradise" when compared with Diane's. Moreover, the priest did not know Diane's name and referred to her only as "the niece." The caseworker then concludes that the priest's information about the Worth household "was not all that good."

After mulling over the information she received during the visit, the caseworker comes to feel that some doubt has been cast on the stories of the priest, the principal, and the Worths' long-term assistance worker. They "may be mistaken." Doubt has also been cast on the moral character of Betty: she may have lied. Some doubt also has been cast on the completely negative evaluation of Mr. Worth's character. As a consequence of her re-interpretation of previously introduced elements, and of her interpretation of new information that suggests alternative explanations of previously introduced elements, the caseworker decides not to apprehend Diane yet.

Further discrepancies appear when members of the household discuss the beating Jennifer was officially interpreted to have received. Mrs. Worth, returning to a position midway between her stance over the telephone on Saturday and her stance in the hospital on that day, denied that her husband had caused all of Jennifer's injuries (as against the accounts of Jennifer and Betty). Her present account was supported by Abe Jr., Kent, and Diane. Diane's position is of particular interest since Betty claimed that the former had run to her on Saturday with the story of the beating. Most significantly, Kent himself stated that he had struck Jennifer over the head with a board – and supplied a motive for doing so. In the context of play among teenagers, this motive appears plausible to the caseworker.

I suggested earlier that since the official definition of the setting of an account determines the interpretation given to the account, the account is indicative of the official perception of the setting. However, a corollary of this assumption returns the interpretation to the initial assumption of the meaningful relation: for according to the official definition of setting, there must be an authoritative account that transcends the context or setting of its telling, if the constructed case is to stand as an objective rendition of the instance it represents. Therefore the caseworker can interpret Mrs. Worth's behaviour in a way that accommodates both her denial in the hospital and her affirmation within her own household that her husband was not completely responsible, if this accommodation pointed to a fruitful line of inquiry. Of couse, this warrant is itself a function of an organizational context, but officials will represent its product as an authoritative account.

In the discussion at the Worth home, some doubts are cast on Betty's and Jennifer's accounts and on Betty's moral character. Therefore if the caseworker is to continue to accept completely their version, she must consider why the other children with whom she spoke and who, according to Jennifer, are beaten by their father, protect him. In other words, she must continue to seek out the motivations of the persons she deems relevant to her interpretation. One possible motivational gloss was supplied by the Worth's long-term assistance officer who said that the family had a reputation for solidarity. But if this is so, then why are Betty and Jennifer excluded from these sentiments of family unity? On the other hand, if Betty and Jennifer are lying, what motive do they have for doing so?

It should be stressed that the interpretation the caseworker builds about the connections between behaviour and motivation are not explicated through a conscious and systematic matching of the compatibility of different elements. Rather, they are perceived and become relevant in a piecemeal fashion during her deliberations and discussions. But they always appear to be perceived as fragments of a larger picture that is assumed to exist. Therefore while pieces of the puzzle may always be lacking, or may acquire different configurations of meaning, whatever information *is* available for interpretation will become the basis for delineating the boundaries of the larger picture (namely, the problem to be solved) which officials assume can be objectified.

Event V: In the Office, Monday, September 30
The caseworker went to Family Court to request a hearing for Jennifer to be made a temporary ward. The date was set for October 4th, four days later. Meanwhile Mrs. Worth went to the office and said that her husband had a job arranged (she mentioned the name of a large company). But Mr. Worth felt that if the police came to question him at work, he would rather not go there at all because he would be too embarrassed. The caseworker urged Mrs. Worth to tell him to go to work "... because it would be in his favour to say he was now employed. He could then *defend himself* by saying that he had been extremely *frustrated* by being home all the time." The caseworker also told her that for the time being Diane could remain with the Worths but that a close check on their behaviour toward Diane would be maintained. Also Diane would have to attend school regularly.
Commentary: The Reconstruction of Character
Once the caseworker begins to perceive discrepancies in the accounts of the accusers, she begins to worry about the fate of the accused. Although she still believes that Mr. Worth beat Jennifer, she is uncertain as to which of her injuries are his responsibility, and whether he should be punished through every available recourse – first through the apprehension of Jennifer, followed by criminal prosecution for assault.

When Mrs. Worth says that Mr. Worth has a job, the caseworker seizes this information to construct an alibi for Mr. Worth's assumed abusive behaviour. This supplied motive does not absolve him of what he is assumed to have done, but it does suggest why, in the present, the pressure that drove him to child abuse would no longer be relevant. According to this motive, he beat Jennifer because he was frustrated, and he was in this state because he was unemployed. A further implication is that the prime cause of his behaviour is not so much within his personality, but within the emasculating state of unemployment and being home much of the time. Then, in his frustration, he might well strike out at a nearby person, who could easily be one of his many children. I might note that the association of socio-economic deprivation with experiences of stress and frustration as a cause of child abuse is commonly found in the "psychologizing" literature on the subject (cf. Gil, 1973:138–9). Therefore the supplied motive is probably contained in the stock of knowledge of the caseworker. If Mr. Worth were working, the major cause of his frustration would no longer be relevant. He would be a reconstituted person who could "defend himself" if he were prosecuted on a criminal charge.

An additional implication of the supplied motive suggests that the caseworker rejects much of the evaluation of Mr. Worth's character supplied by the welfare officer in 1966. One further element becomes relevant in retrospect. When the Worth children were returned to their parents in 1967, the welfare officer stressed that the household had to be kept under close and constant supervision. Yet from 1967 until 1969, there is not a single entry in the case record to indicate that the well-being of the children was kept under surveillance. This may indicate incompetence; it may indicate fear in that caseworkers may avoid visiting homes when they believe the parents are violent (unless strongly pressured to do so by their supervisor); or it may indicate an implicit acknowledgement by the caseworker in 1967 that she overstated the case against Mr. Worth, particularly after the foster homes were unable to manage the children.

Of course, if the caseworker begins to alter retrospectively her interpretation of household biography, then according to the assumptions of meaningful relation and the reach for consistency, she must also re-arrange the components of the problem to make them intelligible as a representation of the instance. For the time being she accomplishes this adjustment by predicating a basic change in Mr. Worth's character upon a future change in his employment situation. Sequentially the latter should occur before he appears in court, if the motive is to be intelligible and viable in that context. The caseworker states that it would be unfortunate if Mr. Worth were to be prosecuted right after his many years of unemployment have ended.

During the period that Mr. Worth's character is undergoing a measure of re-evaluation, the organizational life-world still requires that the case be brought to summation and disposition. Setting the date of the hearing for October 4th, only four days away, is a clear contravention of the Child Welfare Act, 1972. Article 10 (2) states that, "The director or a welfare officer ... shall, at least ten days prior to the date set for the hearing of that application, notify the child's parents ... [of] the time and place of the hearing of the application.''

Event VI: On the Telephone, Tuesday, October 1
In conversation with the caseworker, Mrs. Worth stated that before all the foregoing events she had gone to Family Court to set a hearing for a separation from her husband, because he had forced her to forge checks for him. The hearing had been set for September 23. But then the apprehension of Jennifer occurred, and she felt unable to leave him. She added that Mr. Worth was now working, but that he was afraid of being fired because of the incident with Jennifer. The caseworker asked Mrs. Worth how her husband could suddenly go to work after being judged medically unfit for so many years. She replied that his doctor said it would be good for his "nerves."

Commentary: The Indefinite Elaboration of Accounts
In her attempt to establish a consistent line of interpretation to render the construction of the case intelligible, the caseworker encounters further difficulties. Mrs. Worth states that she did plan to leave her husband; this coincides with Betty's account. Her admitting that her husband forced her to forge checks also supports Betty's account. However, Mrs. Worth has made Betty out to be a "liar," a typification compatible with the case-record description of Betty. Yet there are doubts now about the validity of the case record. If Betty is a liar, then how can she tell the truth? If she is telling the truth, what does this say about Mr. Worth's character, particularly since Mrs. Worth reports that he is now working, an element consistent with his wife's description of his good intentions? In the *process* of bureaucratic interpretation, the establishment of truth and falsehood are central. But these typifications are shown to be highly relative and variable, acquiring their authoritative stature when the outcome of a case is finally decided for bureaucratic purposes. As Silverman and Jones maintain: "... the indefinite elaboration of accounts [is resolved] only by employing practices designed to further practical outcomes. For bureaucracies ... require authoritative accounts of events; a requirement which is satisfied by adopting various procedures to 'close' the infinite features of any interaction ..." (1973:89).

For the caseworker the closure of the indefinite elaboration and re-interpretation of accounts will occur arbitrarily when the court hearing intervenes. Until then she will continue to search for 'what really happened,' even though this may have no bearing on the judicial outcome of the case. This indicates that the organization of interpretations retains its sense of hypothetical relevance until a bureaucratic mechanism specifies closure of the case. But I would suggest that there is a deeper, emotive satisfaction for the caseworker in arriving at an intelligible truth, given the positivist, cause-and-effect thinking which appears to dominate so much of Western, and certainly, bureaucratic perception.

The reaction of the caseworker expresses her ambivalence to the story-line she has been building: she decides not to report the check forgeries to the relevant authorities ("it's not my department") after Mrs. Worth assures her that the victim is being reimbursed. She does not want to punish Mr. Worth. But her suspicion is evident when she inquires how Mr. Worth can suddenly go to work. In reply, Mrs. Worth supplies a motive inspired by an authority: the doctor says that it will be good for his nerves. The full significance of "nerves" is not grasped by the caseworker (I will allude to this later).

Event VII: In the Office, Wednesday, October 2

Mrs. Worth, her oldest daughter, Mary, and her oldest son, Abe Jr., visited the caseworker. They discussed Betty's accusations against her father. Mrs. Worth could not understand how, if Betty thought her father to be such a "monster," she had left her baby in his home when she went to Manitoba for a number of months. They again raised the fact of her attempted suicides and both agreed that she was a "troublemaker" and "liar."

Mrs. Worth produced a note she said Betty had written to her father. The note threatened that, if Jennifer were not taken into care (wardship), Betty would act to have all his children apprehended "by the welfare, *like I had done before*." Mrs. Worth refused to turn this note over to the caseworker, stating that they planned to hire a lawyer to defend Mr. Worth and the lawyer would need the note.

Then Mrs. Worth produced a letter written by Mr. Worth to the caseworker. He began:

I would like very much to come in and see you, to give you my side of the story. because I guess you would understand. and would know different. but it is not only you when it comes to a hearing. they cant affort to face the thruth. because I have faced the same problem before. through lies and apparently they knew it was lies and I was the one that had to pay. and that was it ...

Then he recounted how his children were apprehended in 1966:

but I was caught right off guard. I was home when the welfare worker, [name], and two RCMP officers came. there was an awful going on. that woman even tried to get me to hit her. so she would have me in a tangle. and I wasn't allowed to open my mouth one way or the other. but she never seen her mistake and realized the facts. until it was too late ...

He described how, after his children were placed in foster homes, they did their utmost to return to his home. "The one I was supposed to be after Beating threatened to burn down [name] house so she could get home and she even put off false fire alarms ...'' Finally all the older children ran away and returned to the Worths. "So I don't imagine if I was so hard that they would do that. I would be going the other way.'' Then, he maintained, the caseworker realized her error and returned the younger children as well. Turning to the incident with Jennifer, he writes:

I did give Jennifer a few cuts with the belt. I will admit to that. because things were going very bad and kent and jennifer were fighting over Bottles which has happened a hundred times But they tells me there was a cut on her head. which I found out that kent hit her with a piece of clapboard, and there were other youngsters there and seen it. but I guess jennifer went to the right one when she went to betty. because she would tell her anything to say to get back at me. because a couple of days before that I had to kick them out (Betty and her husband) ...

He related how Betty had once brought a married man to live in the Worth home, and how he had thrown them out. Betty later returned with a girl, to whom he gave his own bed. Then Betty brought in another married man, but fooled him into thinking the man was single. When he found out the truth it was too late for Betty was carrying the man's child. But he threw them out, and Betty went to Manitoba while he looked after the child. More recently he had thrown out Betty and her husband.

He ended the letter with his financial problems: he owed $1800 to a large local furniture and appliance store, a debt he could not meet from his welfare payments. But now that he was permanently employed, he would be able to settle his money difficulties. However, the matter of Jennifer and his possible prosecution menaced him:

I done some searching for this job. I will never get the same chance again, because apparently now I will lose it through this misunderstanding. because if they go progging around and I have to stay off through any cause my job is gone. so I guess thats what will happen. so then I loses my furniture and beds and everything else. then both me and my family our lives are ruined. so a few lies could cause an awful lot of damage. and it seems to me like no one cares as long as they got the atorothy to do you.

Commentary: The Search for Motivation
The perceived discrepancies between the elements of this event and those of previous interpretations indicate again the importance of the search for motivation in order to make the story-line intelligible. In re-reading the case record the present caseworker has a partial impression that in 1966 the previous caseworker awaited a pretext to apprehend the children. But how destructive could the home environment have been then, if all the children of speaking age created a good deal of havoc in order to be returned to their parents? A further discrepancy is introduced by the speed with which Child Welfare redefined the parents after their children created chaos in their foster homes. The reclassification was inspired by the fact that the Worths rebuilt their home, an indication of a change in the characters of the parents. Another possible discrepancy in the story-line concerns Betty's motivation in the note allegedly written to her father. She implies that she

"got him" then, and she threatens to do so again. Perhaps she lied in accusing her father in 1966, and if so, might she not have lied in accusing her father a second time?

Given the assumptions of meaningful relation and the search for consistency, a hypothetical alteration in one aspect of the constructed story-line reverberates throughout this structure. Thus, if Betty lied in 1966, then so did Mary, since at that time they were the most important witnesses against their father. But if Mary lied then, what is she doing now in supporting her father against Betty? Whether the caseworker decides that both Betty and Mary were telling the truth in 1966, or whether she decides that both were lying, some aspect of the constructed story-line in the present will be weakened.

Mr. Worth's account of the beating of Jennifer now corresponds quite well with Kent's account except for the sequence of actions. According to Kent's account, he struck Jennifer first and then his father struck her. According to Mr. Worth's account, he struck Jennifer with the belt after she quarrelled with Kent. At any rate, the accounts of Mr. Worth and Kent are diametrically opposed to those of Jennifer and Betty, except for the element of the belt.

A further discrepancy involves Betty's attitude to her father. If she thought him such a "monster," then why did she leave her baby with him? The caseworker comments: "I wouldn't leave my illegitimate daughter with him if I suspected he beat the children."

The caseworker is prepared now to accept that, hypothetically, Betty has a motive, and perhaps a history of motives, for impugning her father. But if Betty has such a motive, then Jennifer must have one as well, since her account is the most damaging to her father. The caseworker suggests that "perhaps Betty incited Jennifer" to elaborate on the way her father beat her. If this direction in the hypothetical story-line is the true one, then two additional items gain relevance in retrospect. According to Betty's account, some of the Worth children, as well as Diane, rushed to tell her that Mr. Worth was beating Jennifer. These children denied that they did so. Betty said that she telephoned the police, and when they refused to come, nothing happened until Jennifer herself "escaped" about an hour later. Then Betty did nothing after calling the police, either because she was not really concerned (as against the motivation she displayed in the hospital), or perhaps she was afraid of her father. Did she telephone the police at all? If not, did anyone inform her of the beating before Jennifer arrived? The second item concerns the seriousness of Jennifer's injuries. After she had been washed and cleanly dressed in the hospital, "Jennifer looked so much better." Then how much of the appearance of injury was due to her dirty and bedraggled state?

It should be clear why, once the interpretation of an instance is perceived as problematic, the nature of the assumptions that constitute 'official work' can spawn a host of hypothetical story-lines that are more-or-less intelligible solutions. In the end most solutions have a 'more-or-less' validity which is made final only by procedures of bureaucratic closure.

The discovery of Mr. Worth's debt leads the caseworker to re-think the meaning of his going to work, and the meaning of his wife's initial presentation of her difficulties with him, which were also reported by Betty. The Worths' long-term assistance worker related that before the incident with Jennifer, Mrs. Worth came to request assistance with board and lodging, since she had decided to leave her husband. The welfare officer replied that she could not be issued such funds until the department received proof of a legal separation. In order to establish the legality of the separation, Mrs. Worth set a date for a hearing in Family Court. In the meantime the incident concerning Jennifer occurred and Mrs. Worth did not set a new date for a hearing.

This leads the caseworker to doubt strongly that the Worths were ever separated, or that they intended a separation. Instead, she understands the presentation of separation as a tactic to simulate the division of the household in order to obtain additional monies for the whole family while Mrs. Worth lived at home or with a relative, the motivation being their desperate need for money. Initially, the separation was interpreted by the hospital social worker and by the caseworker to mean that Mrs. Worth was "terrified" of her husband. In turn, this interpretation supported the interpretation of Mr. Worth as a beater and abuser. However, in retrospect, the caseworker now believes that the intended separation was a ploy which was simply mistimed, and which was then exploited by Betty to blacken her father's character.

Mr. Worth's large debt of $1800 leads the caseworker to believe that he has been working for a long time. (His announcement of a chance for work and then the fact of his working, both communicated by his wife, were meant to place him in a more favourable light for the relevant officials.) The caseworker reasons as follows: once a person goes on welfare, particularly long-term assistance, large firms cut off credit to him, since he no longer has the expected means of payment. Therefore Mr. Worth could not have received $1800 in credit unless he could have given an employer as a reference. Also, the longer a person is on welfare, the less prepared employers are to hire him, particularly for a permanent position (which Mr. Worth claims he has) since they are less likely to trust his employable capacities. According to this line of interpretation, Mr. Worth has been working, but not reporting his monthly earnings to the Department as he is required to do by law. Now that he admits to working, he will have to report his earnings, and he will have his assistance reduced or stopped, meaning less money for the household.[12] However, he was willing to forego the money in order "to look good": to show that he was following the advice of the hospital social-worker and of the caseworker. By doing so, he may also have found an excuse, a motive, not to appear at the court hearing, since he stated that he would lose his job if he missed work.

The caseworker concludes that if her inferences are correct, Mr. Worth is financially a "desperate man." If he had bought furniture and appliances on credit, he must have sold them, since all his home contained now was a broken-down chesterfield, a few beds, and a battered chrome table and chairs. The supervisor's response to the caseworker's interpretation of the separation, Mr. Worth's work, and their financial plight is, "if they show so much family solidarity, they can't be all that bad." Hence, through a different set of interpretations, they return to the original typification of the household as it was communicated, for quite different reasons, on September 20th by the long-term assistance worker.

In following this line of interpretation, the caseworker and supervisor become worried about Mr. Worth's receiving a fair hearing. Mr. Worth is "not eloquent" whereas the judge "comes on pretty strong sometimes ... he's a little man who sits up there on three piles of s..shugar!" If the hearing should turn up evidence of assault, criminal charges could be brought against Mr. Worth. So they decide to tell the Worths to be represented in court by counsel, for Mr. Worth's own protection. Indicative of a further change in sentiment toward Mr. Worth, the caseworker decides to visit the Worths, unaccompanied, because she is certain that Mr. Worth will not attack her.

Event VIII: In the Worth Home, Thursday, October 3rd
The caseworker visited the Worths and met Mr. Worth for the first time. He was in tears. He again admitted to striking Jennifer with the belt because she had been fighting with Kent. After Kent struck her with the board, no one noticed any blood because it must have been hidden by her hair. He said that then he left the house to search for spare parts for his car, and did not return until 3 P.M. He admitted that if Jennifer had come home from hospital that Saturday, after accusing him, he probably would have been so angry that he would have "killed her." He continued, "and you'll probably put that in your report and hold it against me."[13]

The caseworker raised the matter of the extensive bruising of Jennifer's face, chest, and limbs. With regard to Jennifer's bruised and swollen eye, the Worths could not recall that she had a "black eye" because "all of us have black around the eye." Apparently a number of the Worths, including Mary, although not Betty, had black, smudge-like markings about the eyes, which may have been a symptom of a thyroid condition.

The caseworker warned the Worths to retain a lawyer to represent them at the hearing. They said they would get "the best in town," mentioning the name of a well-known and respected lawyer. Mrs. Worth added that in 1966 her husband had been "wrongfully accused" and that "this will not be repeated." Therefore the caseworker expected the hearing to be postponed either because the Worths would request time to obtain counsel, or because they would appear with counsel, and this would require the department to obtain legal representation.

During her visit the caseworker noted that all the Worth children were around the house, playing with many friends from the neighbourhood. The Worth children "looked contented" and were quite "open" with her. Finally she noted that although the children, including Jennifer, were considered undernourished, the family always had a hot meal in the evening, even if it consisted only of a large bowl of soup. She commented, "In many of my foster homes you may be able to eat off the floor, but is there anything on the table?"

Commentary: Further Interpretations and the Justification of the Organizational Life-World

Retrospectively, Mr. Worth has supplied a motive for striking Jennifer, as well as for his absence later that day when the incident came to the attention of the hospital. The caseworker compares his account with her own experience as a child and with her many years of living in rural southeastern Newfoundland. She remembers that her own father was a firm disciplinarian. And in rural Newfoundland striking children, or cuffing them, was common; "... they used kindling – that leaves splinters – to spank children."[14] By Child Welfare standards, she thinks her own father would have been perceived as a "child beater."

The caseworker perceives Mr. Worth's emotional expression (tears, anger) as consistent with that of a chagrined parent. Moreover, his declaration ("I would have killed her") is compared for authenticity with her own experiences as a parent. She admits to moments in rearing her children that would be comparable to Mr. Worth's sentiments.

The presence of neighbourhood children in the Worth home leads the caseworker to wonder whether their parents would permit them to play in the Worth home if Mr. Worth were a child beater. Moreover, the contented appearance of the Worth children makes the caseworker think that their motive for supporting their father's account of the Jennifer incident was because they liked him.

The caseworker re-thinks Jennifer's physical condition when she was brought to the hospital. Then the doctor considered her "malnourished." But the worker perceives more nutritional content on the Worth table than in many foster homes. Furthermore, and in retrospect, Jennifer said that she had not been fed on the day of the incident, but it had occurred just before midday, and so this was not unusual.

I noted earlier, with reference to the supervisor's description of Jen-

nifer's laceration, that the halo effect in interpretation functioned to expand
the relevance of inference so that lacunae in the search for consistency
could be made explicable and relevant to a developing story-line. In re-
evaluating Jennifer's physical condition, the caseworker recognizes this
for she comments that by describing the laceration as "2 centimeters in
length, the doctor makes it sound longer than 7/8 of an inch." Furthermore,
it required only a single suture and probably would have healed easily by
itself.

The nature of the weapon used is also considered in the light of 'what
happened' and is typified in terms of the kind of person who would likely
use the weapon. Jennifer claims her father struck her with a high-heeled
shoe, whereas Kent claims he, himself, struck her with a board. After
meeting Mr. Worth the caseworker comments that she cannot see Mr.
Worth using a high-heeled shoe because "he's not that type of man."

As more discrepancies are perceived, the caseworker is forced to re-
evaluate further those themes that were made relevant to her construction
of the story-line. Earlier she had re-interpreted Jennifer's accusation
against her father and concluded that Betty might have incited the girl. In
addition, Betty was shown to have a plausible motive for doing so, and
possibly a history of such motives. Now, after her visits to the Worth home,
the caseworker also questions Jennifer's motive for her explanation of why
her father beat her. Jennifer said that her father beat her because her room
was untidy. The caseworker describes the house as being dirty, untidy, and
almost empty of furniture. She says to the supervisor, "There's more junk
on their kitchen table than on your desk right now." The house also
"smells." (My own impression is that caseworkers use visual, tactile, and
olfactory criteria, in that order, to rank the extent to which a home is
perceived as "clean" or "dirty.") The introduction of olfactory perception
suggests that the caseworker considers the home to be "dirty." Therefore
if the house was dirty, would Mr. Worth become upset at untidiness and
strike out at Jennifer in particular, seeing as all the children shared one
room? Descriptions of the home in the case record, and the caseworker's
own perceptions, suggest not. Thus a motive that sounded plausible in the
hospital setting becomes suspect, and perhaps, inauthentic, in the context
of the home.

Before summarizing the positions of the supervisor and the caseworker
on the day before the hearing, a cautionary note is in order about the nature
of interpretation and inference. The halo effect of inference cements the
gaps between meaningful relations and so provides what appears to be a
more solid foundation, which can be perceived as internal consistency. At
some point, the persons who are making this construction begin to treat it
as a reality that not only connects various relevant themes and elements,
but that itself becomes a source of information fitting into the emerging

pattern. Thus plausible elements can be added to the construction even though an explicit warrant for this addition does not exist in the available verbal or documentary accounts. In effect, the evaluators themselves have difficulty in keeping track of the level of their inference and its points of attachment to the accounts they have received.

One example of this occurs when the supervisor and caseworker are trying to account for the source of Jennifer's injuries. Explanations have been received for the scalp laceration, a mark that appears to have been caused by a belt blow, and the 'black eye.' Then the letter written by Mr. Worth to the caseworker states that he admitted slapping Jennifer, "but not all that much." Though not explicit, it does appear to be an attempt to account for the other bruises on Jennifer's face and chest. In other words, and in accordance with the assumption of consistency, the officials use the letter as a warrant to extend their inference and to account for as many aspects of the instance as is feasible. But they are not aware that in the process, they are losing their actual warrant for doing so and instead, they are maintaining a hypothetical warrant – a 'guess' – which they are trans-forming into a reality.

On the day before the hearing, the caseworker and supervisor are no longer certain of 'what really happened.' The supervisor maintains that, "they've been caught out in *lying* since this thing started – I hate these family affairs where everybody is at everybody and covering up for everyone ... We don't know what happened. Its all *hearsay*, anyway, and they're changing their stories about. All we can do is tell the judge that we're presenting witnesses *to establish what did happen*, and then let him take it from there." The supervisor confirms implicitly that they have failed to establish a single authoritative account of 'what happened.' But she reaffirms her faith in the organizational life-world – in this case at the hearing – to come up with such an account.

However, there is a subtle difference of interest between the ways in which the child workers and the court use the gloss about 'what really happened.' This difference is easily obscured by the gloss, and the differ-ence will deny the child workers their final account, even though they will be given an authoritative official verdict that will close the case, at least until the next event.

Throughout their investigation the caseworker and supervisor have been concerned to establish who did what to whom, and why. But, as Van Stolk (1972:54) has pointed out, the purpose of court hearings in Canada gener-ally is "... not to prove that the child was beaten by a particular individual, but only to point out that in the light of medical and social findings, the child has not been properly cared for." Thus the relevant question that will be before the court is what happened to whom. Phrased this way the interest of the court is problematic for the child workers in three respects: first, the investigative stance requires that a cause be linked to an effect. Second, when so much information derives from accounts about accounts (from hearsay), the location of the prime cause within a person depends upon the evaluators' being able to typify the motivation and reasoning of this person. The ascription of motivation to a person also endows him with the recognition of will: he could have chosen to do something else, unless there were extenuating circumstances. If the location of such a person is crucial to establish cause-and-effect, then once the location is hypothetically accomplished, the person cannot be dropped from the configuration and the relevant question be rephrased in more passive terms. For the person, as the cause, is crucial in enabling cause-and-effect, as a meaningful relation, to maintain its coherence. Third, once the court renders its verdict, the child worker will have to work with the person(s) who is(are) presumed, although not stated, to have been the causal agents of neglect/abuse. Then the worker will have to presume again that someone is a causal agent without necessarily having the final word specifying the accountability of this person.

Since the supervisor had little contact with the protagonists of the case, she perceives them as contemporaries rather than 'consociates.' Contemporaries are experienced as typical in their behaviour and motivation whereas the consociate is experienced "... as a unique individual in his unique biographical situation" (Jehenson, 1973:221). However, from the case worker's viewpoint, whose case it is, and who had comparatively frequent contact with the protagonists, she is not content to typify them as liars maintaining their official reputation for family solidarity.

She thinks that "Abe" (as she now calls him) "is capable of hitting his kids, but not out of cruelty." His mistake was that (a) he hit "too hard," and (b) his action was reported. She is now prepared to recognize the sensitizing effect of the incident with Diane. She states that had it not occurred when it did in the sequence of events, or if it had been cleared up the same day instead of after the Jennifer incident, the reaction of Child Welfare to the latter incident would have been much less severe. In other words, she is prepared to recognize that "... two not very firm opinions might well add up to 'reasonable belief'" (Paulsen, 1973:173).

Thus a sequence of events developed that contained the emerging constraints that prevented the caseworker from arriving at a fully intelligible and satisfactory story-line. The Friday event left the caseworker "on edge," and influenced the speed with which Jennifer was apprehended on Saturday. In turn this speedy apprehension limited the time available in which to construct a satisfactory organizational account. Therefore the point in time at which the caseworker changed many of her opinions about the Worths is also the point at which the case will be finally evaluated in terms of typifications applied to it nearly two weeks before.

The caseworker states that she is no longer certain what did happen, but that she finds the following scenario the most "logical": Kent struck Jennifer with a board, and then Mr. Worth struck her with a belt. But she still thinks that Jennifer should be removed from the home because family relationships are poor and should be given a chance to "cool down." As well, if Jennifer were left in the home, she, like Betty before her, would probably continue to threaten her father with "you got out of it this time; but wait until next time."

During the previous twelve days the caseworker has moved from a position of concern for Jennifer to a position of concern, almost equally as strong, for the protection of the father. Of course, the above justification for requesting temporary wardship is related to a diffuse and ambiguous conception of family relationships that is not covered by the Child Welfare Act, but that can be made intelligible in terms of the occupational knowledge and related typified concerns of the caseworker.

An implication of the caseworker's current position is that Jennifer (and Betty) probably lied in part about the nature and extent of the beating she received from her father. The supervisor who states that a parent should never strike a child still accepts Jennifer's story in principle. She introduces a further typification to make intelligible her position: that a daughter of that age would never lie about her father, or attempt to manipulate him, in so "serious" a matter. Here the supervisor has recourse to the assumption that the official definition of the setting or context of action determines its interpretation. The supervisor (and the caseworker) perceive the instance of the beating, and its likely consequences, as "serious"; therefore it is so for the purpose of ascribing motivation to Jennifer and of inferring how she would behave in accordance with that ascription. How Jennifer perceives her intention toward her father is indeterminate and irrelevant for the purpose of interpreting the problem.

The caseworker has difficulty accepting the supervisor's reasoning. For her Jennifer is not "a girl of that age" but a consociate whose position can be determined only in relation to the other protagonists and the relationships among them. But, states the supervisor, "if Jennifer did do something like this, then it only shows that something is really wrong somewhere in that family, and Jennifer should be removed anyway."

At the outset, the relevance of themes and elements was said to be problem-oriented (following Schutz and Luckmann). They were perceived as bearing on the explication of the instance in varying degrees. According to the assumption of meaningful relation, officials constructed the meaning of the case so that it exhibited internal consistency and was intelligible to the organizational life-world. But the very construction of the case contained constraints on the way these officials could come to perceive it. Working within their construction they could not destroy it when it appeared as a less intelligible rendering of the problem. The case that was built on a connected set of assumptions and interpretations begins to acquire reality, such that any further interpretations must be explicated in terms of the boundaries of relevance already in place. These are the limits of the elasticity of relevance.

The constructed case becomes the real case which in turn limits the range of relevant interpretations that are permitted in the light of additional elements. So, although the supervisor and caseworker disagree about the most likely story-line, the case as a construction of reality (but as distinct from 'what really happened') leads them to the same conclusion: that temporary wardship should be granted to Jennifer. The supervisor admits that even if the caseworker's version is the correct one, within the boundaries of relevance that were established, there is only one proper outcome if the relevance of the organizational life-world itself is to be maintained and justified. They will be dissatisfied with the hearing precisely because there will remain a serious discrepancy between the constructed case as a simulation of reality that is organizationally intelligible on the one hand, and 'what really happened' as a representation of their wider life-worlds on the other. Thus, they are on the brink of perceiving the arbitrary nature of the construction of their organizational life-world.

Event IX: In Court, Friday, October 4

Before the hearing the caseworker, still concerned with what really happened, tried to impress upon Jennifer the importance of telling the truth in court since she would be sworn in to give testimony. The caseworker noted later that, "I thought now we might really get at the truth." Mr. Worth did not come, ostensibly because he was at work, but Mrs. Worth, her daughter Mary, and Mary's husband did appear. The Worths were not represented by a lawyer. But the judge stated that if they agreed to wardship there was no need for counsel. Since the sole judicial concern was to establish whether the child had been neglected, no hearsay evidence was introduced.

The first witness was the caseworker. Asked to describe the condition of the Worth home, she said that it was untidy, rather than dirty or filthy, since she felt the judge would hold these evaluations against the Worths. The hospital doctor testified next that the instance was possible child abuse; he mentioned the scalp laceration, a bruised and swollen eye, and a large raised welt across the upper arm and chest. The hospital social-worker testified about Jennifer's emotional state when she was brought to the hospital.

Then Jennifer testified without being sworn in. Her testimony lasted perhaps one and a half minutes. The judge asked her if she wanted to return home. She shook her head. He then asked her if she wanted to see her mother again. She nodded. Asked whether she wanted to see her brothers and sisters again, she nodded. Asked whether she wanted to see her father, she shook her head. The judge asked Mrs. Worth if she consented to temporary wardship and she replied that she did. The judge stated that the only purpose of the hearing was to establish neglect, that there was a point where discipline became cruelty, and at this point the child had to be removed. He granted temporary wardship for twelve months with visiting rights.

Whereas no evidence of the cause of neglect was presented, the judge recorded whatever details were testified to, and the record would then be admissible as evidence were Mr. Worth to be prosecuted on criminal charges. The next step was for the supervisor to prepare a report on the case for the Director of Child Welfare, who would pass it in turn to the Department of Justice with a recommendation of whether or not to press charges against Mr. Worth.

Commentary: Bureaucratic Dissatisfactions

No testimony was taken as to who caused the injuries suffered by Jennifer. But there appears to have been a tacit agreement about Mr. Worth's beating her, and hence the remarks of the judge about the line between discipline and cruelty. For the supervisor and caseworker, the concretizing of the case and its official recording and disposition would have been more satisfactory if *cause* had been officially identified, in addition to *effect*, since the application of their stock of knowledge to an explication of the instance had been predicated upon assumptions of cause-and-effect. These enabled them to investigate the instance in a manner intelligible to their organizational life-world. The rendering of the verdict solely on the effects – the injuries – led the supervisor to comment that "the child might have fallen over the stairs." Put simply, without including the component of motivation located in a person, the explanation of the case made little sense; however, she did agree that the verdict was correct.

After the hearing, the caseworker still has her doubts about who was responsible. She feels that the judge was "high-handed with his power," and "I would much rather have Abe for a father than the judge." Finally, she doubts whether the organizational life-world can investigate and resolve instances of the typification "suspected neglect/abuse" in a manner satisfactory to itself and to the wider life-world. She states: "If we had to clamp down on child-beating in Newfoundland, we'd have to clamp down on half the population." In other words, the simulated construct of the case bears only a limited resemblance to instances that occur in the wider life-world and that are considered problematic in those terms. Even though the organizational life-world has produced a conclusive label for the instance (for the time being), it nevertheless has failed to penetrate the reality of the wider life-world as it affects the protagonists of the case. She argues that the Worths did not retain a lawyer for the hearing because "people are terribly afraid of losing their social assistance, and since they are already at the bottom of the barrel, they are cowed, meek, and submissive." For her the explication of the instance has been the solution of an organizational problem rather than of a real one.

CONCLUSION

The most evident facet of the case through time is the massive shift in sentiment towards the protagonists as experienced by the caseworker: she ends the first phases of her investigation by inferring that the story-line concerns a father who cruelly beat his daughter; she concludes her inquiries uncertain as to what really happened. But she continues to assert the relevance of the organizational life-world to the case by suggesting that since family relationships are so poor, it would be better for all concerned if Jennifer were removed for a period.

In their attempts to elucidate the story-line of the case, the caseworker and her supervisor work through a process of interpretation. Through this process, in accordance with the principle of compatibility, they try to attain consistency in explanation by typifying persons and behaviour. This search for consistency establishes the relevance of elements to the emerging case. By ascribing motives to protagonists, officials make intelligible those behaviours of the former which they perceive as relevant. The cementing of motivation to the elements perceived as relevant enables officials to construct the story-line as a cause-and-effect relationship that substantiates the goals and ideology of the organizational life-world. Moreover, officials try to maintain control over the consistency of the story-line through retrospective interpretation. This permits them to perceive the past in terms of the ongoing present and to re-interpret the past to make it congruent with incoming information.

The bureaucratic interpretations of this case are indefinite and indeterminate until the moment of closure. I would suggest, however, that the development of this case is not an idiosyncratic one but one which proceeds according to assumptions that have much wider currency in the operation of bureaucracy. I am not suggesting that bureaucratic assumptions are not "rational" and "universalistic," but that they are so *in their own light*. The tale of the case is, after all, a bureaucratic story constructed for an organizational audience.

The problematic nature of bureaucratic interpretation in building an intelligible story-line is illustrated further by a datum to which I alluded in the analysis of the case. In 1970, Mr. Worth was pressured by the department to undergo an operation to correct his hernia or else have his long-term assistance suspended. But this threat was not implemented because in

1971, a psychiatrist, associated with a hospital other than the one to which Jennifer was brought, diagnosed Mr. Worth as a "simple schizophrenic." From then on he was treated monthly for his condition, and his mental illness justified the continuation of long-term assistance; he was no longer pressured to undergo surgery.

In reading the case record, the caseworker missed this entry and no one informed her of it. Therefore this information did not enter the interpretation and construction of the story-line of the case. In turn, the caseworker missed the relevance of two hints to Mr. Worth's condition in the information she received. Mrs. Worth's stating that the doctor said work would be beneficial for her husband's nerves, and Mr. Worth's alluding to being sick in his letter were probably references to his officially defined mental state. The caseworker took "nerves" to mean what is widely used in Newfoundland to describe a multitude of conditions; and she misunderstood his being "sick" as a reference to his hernia condition.

In this there is much irony. The official designation of "mental illness," with its implication of personality disorder, would have provided officials with a substantial warrant to construct quite a different role for Mr. Worth in the emerging story-line. For example, if Mr. Worth had been accepted as mentally ill when he struck Jennifer, then according to the assumptions of meaningful relation, the reach for consistency, biographical stretch, and retrospective interpretation, his mental state could have suggested an alternative authoritative account of what happened in 1966. Moreover, given official perception of the gloss of mental illness, it would have provided an alternative authoritative explanation of Mr. Worth's behaviour in the present. Then the gloss of "mental illness" could well have absolved him of personal responsibility for what happened, and there would have been little fear of his being prosecuted on a charge of assault. By the end of the case, this is what the caseworker wanted.

By the end of Event II the majority of elements perceived as relevant to the case have already been introduced (see my Appendix). The pattern of relationship given to these elements also appears to determine the boundaries of relevance that the story-line acquires. Thus the remainder of the case is concerned mainly with the rearrangement of elements introduced in Events I and II to create alternative patterns of meaning and explanation. It is the acceptance of a pattern of meaning that gives the remainder of the investigation a desultory appearance at times. As Zimmerman (1969:349) aptly observes: "The consideration of what may be taken as evidence is never far removed from the costs of securing it." After Event II, the officials are so certain that they have uncovered 'what really happened' that their subsequent awareness of uncertainty appears to occur in a haphazard fashion and this contributes to their passive pursuit of evidence. The establishment of the boundaries of investigative relevance and the way the investigation is pursued are probably connected to the kinds of assumptions with which these officials work.

These assumptions function in interrelated ways to define and integrate the world of meaning that is the "case." Once the gloss of "suspected neglect/abuse" is anchored to specific persons, then the elements of information perceived as connected to these persons and to the alleged instance begin to form the boundaries of relevance of the case. Within these the compatibility of gloss and instance will either be substantiated or disallowed. Thus the boundaries of relevance of the case come into existence once the gloss of suspicion is applied; they are formed by those elements that warranted the introduction of the gloss in the first place.

Within these boundaries, the assumption of meaningful relation requires that the included elements be shown to co-exist in authentic association and not simply in coincidence. Given this assumption, officials begin to search for the connections. Their warrant for this search is the assumption of the permanence of motivation, such that there is always a cause for the effects that constitute the instance for which the gloss of suspicion was first invoked. Thus, officials search for evidence of the motives which led the protagonists to cause the effect that constitutes the instance. In this organizational life-world, motivation is the dynamic which permits officials to show that the elements within the boundaries of relevance are connected in a meaningful way.

Since the product of the investigation should be a structure of explanation that takes the form of cause-and-effect, and since information about elements continues to be perceived during the investigation, the assumption of the reach for consistency plays a major role in managing the accomplishment of congruence among elements that are shown to have different facets of meaning. The management function of this assumption has two aspects. First, it permits officials to juggle different patterns of meaning in their search for the truth – the pattern of meaningful relations most compatible with the instance of suspicion – without necessarily committing themselves to one such pattern. Second, the assumption permits the halo effect of interpretation to gloss over minor inconsistencies or loopholes in the structure of explanation and to establish a more integrated pattern of meaning.

Nevertheless, since the boundaries of relevance of the developing case are permeable to certain kinds of new information, contradictions or discrepancies in explanation pose difficulties. These difficulties weaken the reach for consistency in meaningful relations that should be established if the problem represented by the instance of suspicion is to be resolved satisfactorily. But discrepancy must cast doubt if the assumption of meaningful relation is operative, since this assumption posits that the association of elements in the case is not accidental or coincidental. These difficulties are resolved or smoothed over through time by the continuous reach for consistency.

If the boundaries of relevance of the case are permeable, then the reach for consistency is also elastic; it permits movement over time to uncover evidence that will resolve discrepancy. In this endeavour support is obtained from the assumption of the permanence of motivation, suggesting there is a history to the character and motivation of persons that can illuminate their behaviour in the present. The notion of a personal history permits the assumption of consistency to reach into the past, to dredge for information that may be relevant to meaningful relations being established in the present. In this way present behaviour can be represented as a continuation of past motivation. The construction of a personal history that is relevant to the instance of suspicion is what I have termed biographical stretch. The assumption of biographical stretch permits the temporal triangulation of present and past, to infer what is likely to occur in the future, as this is relevant to a final accounting of the case.

Biographical stretch operates *in tandem* with another aspect of the reach for consistency: the assumption of retrospective interpretation. Once the construction of personal histories opens the door to the past, this passageway remains open for the following reason. The case is constructed through time, so that whatever happened previously on the time-scale relevant to the case is a feature of its history. According to the reach for consistency, alternative patterns of meaning are being juggled during this period until a final one appears. Therefore this assumption must also allow for the alteration of meaning within patterns, to make these patterns more congruent with the final accounting of the case that they purport to explicate. In other words, elements of meaningful relations must often be re-interpreted along the constructed time-line of the case, if the quest for internal consistency is to be accomplished.

When the constructed time and story-lines of the case reach bureaucratic closure, the importance of biographical stretch and retrospective interpretation diminish. Diachrony becomes synchrony as the official truth, which is understood to transcend the context of its telling, is presented to the organizational life-world and to other audiences. The structure of the case is then fully reified according to bureaucratic criteria: a final account of meaningful relations will be entered into official dossiers as an explication and summation of the gloss, ''suspected neglect/abuse.''

Yet it should be clear that to achieve this disposition, officials must engage in a *dialectical* process of interpretation. In this sense, the interpretation of the meaning of elements enables a reified structure of the case to be constructed. In turn, this constructed structure strengthens the boundaries of the relevance of the case and so points to those interpretations that can be construed as more relevant to its solution. Therefore we should consider bureaucratic interpretation to be a dialectic between the interpretation of elements and the emerging structure of a case. This process may well be predicated upon the kinds of assumptions which I have outlined here.

Are the assumptions I identified peculiarly bureaucratic, or are they more general directional devices? I think they are devices related to positivist perception and interpretation, and that in the main, bureaucratic personnel perceive their organizational life-world and its tasks in positivist terms. This is why a phenomenological perspective that assumes the bureaucratic life-world to be an arbitrary but integrated and meaningful social construct can illuminate the interpretive dynamics which enable this life-world to function in accordance with its positivist assumptions about its own procedures and accomplishments. It is the factor of relevance that turns the common-sense reasoning of these assumptions into bureaucratic reasonings. The way in which the elements of the case are chosen and the ways in which they are put together to form patterns of meaning are functions of the relevancies of the organizational life-world. These relevancies tailor the use of assumptions in ways that are designed to replicate the structure of the organizational life-world.

The relevancies of the organizational life-world are thematic, motivational, and interpretable (Schutz and Luckmann, 1973:186–207). The bureaucratic task sets the problem that is to be explicated; that is, the theme or idea of child neglect/abuse is perceived as a problem relevant to child welfare. Legal statutes and department directives enunciate the relevance of this theme for the caseworker. That she/he is motivated to undertake and explicate the case is also set by the bureaucratic task, except when there is doubt as to how well the problem can be handled. She/he then has recourse to a stock of knowledge that derives from the wider life-world (as when our caseworker compared her father to Mr. Worth). When she/he accepts this recourse, she/he begins to perceive how arbitrary the organizational life-world really is. But it is in the domain of interpretive relevance, where the organizational life-world provides so little direction, that the assumptions become particularly relevant; and their positivist features are quite compatible with the way the organization works.

In short, the application of rule to case, in Weber's terms, passes through a landscape of assumptions and interpretations that ostensibly have little to do with the journey, but that, on closer examination, are found to constitute the journey itself.

A final note: as the study of complex and modernizing societies increasingly become the focus of anthropological work, so the study of small-scale bureaucratic processes will become more relevant to anthropological study (cf. Handelman, 1976). These should be met and analysed in their own terms of operation rather than in terms of models of behaviour that are present in much of current anthropological thinking as in, for example, "political man," "economic man," or "maximizing man." To this end, a phenomenological perspective will be illuminating.

NOTES

1   Therapeutic intervention and legal protection often involve diametrically opposed stances in dealing with family members who are suspected of having abused their children. I have lumped them together here because in practice, in order for the adherents of either approach to decide the disposition of a case, they must construct the motivations of the persons involved.

2   One may suggest that although the attribution of motivation is conceived as a psychological delineation by clinicians, and by other members of the helping profession, the act of ascribing motives and their contents is an ideological attribution defined and made relevant in professional terms. Hence although the content of attribution is termed "psychological," its process of ascription is social; and therefore is amenable to social analysis as the routine behaviour of certain categories of persons (see Blum and McHugh, 1971).

3   Gelles (1974) exempts Gil from adhering to a simple linear causative model of child abuse, by suggesting that Gil includes social factors in his model of abuse. Nevertheless, as indicated by Gil's definition of abuse (cited above), he clearly gives primacy to the psychological construct of "intention" in attempting to explain the behaviour of the person labelled "abuser." Moreover, Gil's social factors do not express the contexts within which these behaviours occured, or were evaluated, but only the typifications of these which were amenable to survey analysis.

4   The "psychologizing" professions contain a stock of knowledge which might be characterized as self-generating, in the sense that its typifications tend to exclude themes external to the psyche, while these typifications can be expanded to encompass and explain all aspects of behaviour, through the interpretive medium of the expert. Voysey (1972:541) notes that: "One can see ... how psychiatry can be as powerful a mode of legitimation as religion. All 'external' phenomena and problems are regarded as but the manifestations of internal psychic disorder of some kind. Some clients have more 'inner strength' than others, but all can be helped to react positively and constructively to achieve the main end of 'acceptance.'"

5   I have indulged in certain simplifications here. Clearly the perception and definition of the situation among hospital personnel, social workers, and judges differ according to the different organizational concerns they represent. Still, they have more in common with one another than with the perceptions of their clients. Nevertheless, with regard to judicial proceedings where neglect is defined according to the behaviour of parents, it seems that circumstantial evidence is becoming more important in making a decision. For example, a recent opinion of the Family Court of the State of New York states that: "... the condition of the child speaks for itself, thus permitting an inference of neglect to be drawn from proof of the child's age and condition, and that the latter is such as *in the ordinary course of things does not happen* if the parent who has responsibility and control of an infant is protective and non-abusive" (Paulsen, 1974:155, my emphasis). The circumstantial evidence is based on behavioural attributes that are accepted as integral to the syndrome. Thus the clinical constructs of the adherents of therapeutic intervention may come to have a more powerful effect on the judiciary in the future.

6   Most reported instances occurred within census tracts 5, 6, 7, 10 and 11. According to the 1971 census, the percentage of single-detached dwellings within these tracts were respectively 36, 15, 7, 25, and 47. In comparison, areas outside the inner city (census tracts 12, 13, 14) contained respectively 60, 62, and 67% single-detached dwellings. Another indication of

relative density is found in "persons per room (average)." For census tracts 5, 6, 7, 10, and 11 these figures were respectively .74, .76, .68, .64, .72, whereas for census tracts 12, 13, and 14, they were respectively .76, .52, and .62 (Statistics Canada, 1973).

7   Failure to report is punishable by a $200 fine and/or two months in prison. To the best of my knowledge no one has been prosecuted under Article 49. Hypothetically, parents or caretakers found to have abused their child could be prosecuted on this ground for having failed to report themselves. Where children under the age of ten are found to have been neglected or abused, the Criminal Code of Canada takes precedence over provincial statutes.

8   Child welfare officers in St. John's do investigate every report they receive in contrast to, for example, New York City, where bureaucratic interpretations of the source of a report, and of neglect itself, were apparently aimed at reducing the load of public welfare agencies.

9   Differences in experience would affect, presumably, the kinds of typifications workers find themselves most comfortable with in their investigations.

10   Steinmetz and Strauss (1974:6) reported a nation-wide American survey disclosing that one-third of the respondents had been frequently spanked as children, and nearly all respondents had been spanked at some time. Gil (1973:55), referring to another nation-wide American survey, reported that nearly 60% of respondents, "... thought that anybody could at some time injure a child in his care."

11   Parents themselves may ask that their child be taken into care for a temporary period, usually not exceeding three to six months. Such a 'non-ward' agreement is not legally binding and can be terminated at any time by either party.

12   At this point he had not yet informed his long-term assistance worker of his employment, and the caseworker could not decide whether or not to do so herself.

13   The caseworker did not transcribe this statement into the case record.

14   Information on disciplinary socialization practices in Newfoundland is quite sparse. Szwed (1966:80) writes that: "Children are seldom struck or spanked. On the rare occasion when they are, it is in the parent's anger ...' Faris (1972:76) notes that "... corporal punishment is rare." Both writers are referring to areas of rural Newfoundland different from the one the caseworker lived in.

APPENDIX

The Major Elements of the Case

x – indicates in which Events the element is introduced without a change in its meaning.

R – indicates that the element is re-interpreted.

Elements are listed in roughly the order in which they appear in the case.

	Events							
Elements	I	II	III	IV	V	VI	VII	VIII
1. priest as informant	x			R				
2. Diane drinks, smokes	x		x	R				
3. "murder" in family	x			R				
4. abduction of Diane	x			R				
5. Worth reputation for confrontation (solidarity)	x			x			x	

Elements	Events							
	I	II	III	IV	V	VI	VII	VIII
6. welfare officer as informant	x		x	R				
7. Betty brings Jennifer to hospital		x						
8. Jennifer not fed in morning		x						R
9. Jennifer's room untidy		x						R
10. face beaten		x						
11. struck with shoe		x						R
12. turpentine applied		x						
13. belt blow(s)		x					x	x
14. motivation of Betty		x		R			R	
15. children informing Betty		x		R			R	
16. Betty calls police		x					R	
17. Jennifer's escape		x						
18. car at home		x		R				R
19. forged checks		x	x			x		
20. Mrs. Worth leaving husband		x				x		R
21. Betty's motive for mother		x						
22. Mr. Worth's character		x	x	R	R			R
23. Mrs. Worth's denial (phone)		x		R				
24. Mrs. Worth's defensiveness		x					R	
25. Mrs. Worth's story change		x						
26. Mr. Worth going to work		x			x		R	
27. Mrs. Worth's fear of husband		x					R	
28. head laceration		x		R				R
29. weal on arm		x					x	
30. "psychological trauma"		x						
31. "malnutrition"		x						R
32. children not in school			x					
33. "knifing" in Worth family			x					
34. Abe Jr. bad influence			x	R				
35. Mr. Worth a heavy drinker			x	R				
36. burn on Kent			x					
37. Kent's account				x			R	R
38. Betty's baby							x	
39. Mr. Worth owes $1800							x	
40. behavior of neighborhood children								x
41. behavior of Worth children								x

The Bureaucratization of Anguish: The Workmen's Compensation Board in an Industrial Disaster

3

Elliott Leyton

PREAMBLE

The ethnographic focus of this essay is the impact of a bureaucracy, in this case the Workmen's Compensation Board, on two adjacent rural communities in Newfoundland, which have been devastated by industrial disease. Its theoretical concern is with the process of transformation through which a 'rational' bureaucracy, designed to ameliorate suffering, actually creates as much as it relieves. More generally, the essay is an enquiry into certain aspects of the nature of bureaucracy.

Part of the explanation for the incongruence between objective and accomplishment undoubtedly lies in the ambiguous position the Workmen's Compensation Board (referred to hereafter as the WCB) occupies in Canadian society. Neither government agency nor private corporation, the WCB's fealty is divided between government (which determines its regulations through provincial legislation) and industry (which finances its operations). My concern is not with this dilemma, however, but with that important part of the incongruence which can be traced to an inherent incompatibility between the bureaucratic and traditionalist views* of the world. It is this issue that provides focus and perimeter for the essay.

Such a mandate necessarily entails a brief discussion of the nature of bureaucracy. For Max Weber and his intellectual descendants, bureaucracy was *the* rational and efficient administrative machine; its major characteristics were specialization, a hierarchy of authority, a system of rules, and impersonality.

The decisive reason for the advance of bureaucratic organization has always been its purely technical superiority over any other form of organization. The fully developed bureaucratic mechanism compares with other organizations exactly as does the machine with the non-mechanical modes of production.

Precision, speed, unambiguity, knowledge of the files, continuity, discretion, unity, strict subordination, reduction of friction and of material and personal costs – these are raised to the optimum point in the strictly bureaucratic administration ... (Weber in Gerth and Mills, 1958:214).

No one could accuse Weber of an insensitivity to the potential defects in bureaucratic organization, but Blau (1956:33) has admitted that "since he

---

* By *traditionalist*, I refer simply to the qualities which flow from membership in an ancient culture based on personalized and face-to-face social relations. No associations of backwardness or ignorance are intended.

treats dysfunctions only incidentally, his discussion leaves the impression that administrative efficiency in bureaucracies is more stable and less problematical than it actually is.'' Indeed, so powerful is this impression that the standard sociological reader on bureaucracy (Merton *et al*, 1952) devotes less than 30 of its 464 pages to the pathological aspects of bureaucratic organization. Even there, the assumption is clearly that bureaucracy is a perfectible tool, but sometimes subject to organizational pathologies.

These pathologies seem to be of two major types. The first type, which may be called over-organization, involves an excessive development of those bureaucratic routines which, kept within limits, are functionally necessary to the operation of a large administrative apparatus ... The second type is under-organization. This includes those bureaucratic ills, as instanced by nepotism, favoritism, graft, corruption, and the like, which upon analysis, are found to represent failure to live up to the requirements of bureaucratic structure (Merton *et al*, 1952:396).

In much sociological and popular thought, then, Weber's treatment of the theoretical characteristics of an ideal construct has been vulgarized to the point where ideal characteristics have become actual ones, and potential virtues transformed into inevitable ones. Even if this vulgarization is a step Weber himself never made, it has nevertheless been enshrined in the cosmologies of the industrial middle class.

This essay is concerned specifically with the activities of a bureaucracy staffed by medical and administrative personnel of the highest calibre, which nonetheless behaves as if it had an *irrational* character. This tendency towards irrationality, I argue, is inherent in the structure of bureaucracy when it must deal with traditional and rural sectors of society. Traditionalists have great difficulty in both comprehending and absorbing into their cosmology a system of dispassionate and impersonal regulations, since the ideological mainsprings of traditionalist societies are based upon passionate and personal postulates.

I try to show how each 'rational' bureaucratic decision is seen by the traditionalists as a consequence of either irrational or arbitrary notions attributed to the bureaucracy's medical and administrative officials, or of the traditionalists' personal pressure for the intervention of their patron. Conversely, the behaviour of the traditionalists is regarded by the bureaucrats as a result of ''ignorance of WCB regulations,'' ''lack of faith in WCB personnel,'' and an obsession with maximizing personal financial gain. The contradictory and mutually exclusive cosmologies of traditionalists and bureaucrats create a mutual incomprehensibility which transforms ameliorative intent into destructive consequence. In this special sense, then, bureaucracy does not have a ''rational character,'' there is no coordination of ''means and ends,'' and ''matter of factness'' does not ''dominate its bearing'' (Weber in Gerth and Mills: 244). To the contrary, bureaucracy can be seen as an essentially urban, middle-class, and industrial construct which, in juxtaposition with this traditionalist society, is both source and distributor of anguish and despair. To facilitate this enquiry, after a brief introduction to the devastated villages and the WCB, I examine the confrontation of the two cosmologies, the critical areas of contradiction, and the quality of the encounter between bureaucrat and traditionalist.

St. Lawrence and Lawn

St. Lawrence and Lawn are separated by nine miles of barren ground on the boot of the Burin Peninsula on Newfoundland's south coast. With a combined population of some 3,173 persons distributed among 565 households (1971 Census), they are much larger than conventional Newfoundland outports, their present size being attributable primarily to the proximity of the fluorspar mines that employ 330 miners as well as managerial and support staff.

When the last glacier receded from the St. Lawrence area less than 10,000 years ago, it left behind a hostile and barren environment. Scraped of its soil by the glaciers and cooled by the Labrador current, the land is little more than an extensive treeless bog dotted with innumerable small ponds. But the sea was rich and St. Lawrence became a European summer fishing station by the late 16th century, and a permanent settlement by the beginning of the 19th century. Although the majority of the 'livyers' were Irish and Roman Catholic, a large minority were of English Protestant origin. This minority, with no church to marry or bury them, followed a pattern established elsewhere in Newfoundland: they converted to Catholicism, took on an Irish cultural identity,[1] and consolidated into one traditionalist culture throughout the region.

Throughout the 19th and the first quarter of the 20th centuries, these settlers were traditional, small-scale, inshore fishermen, which most anthropologists would label "peasants": production was intended neither for subsistence purposes nor for the discharge of kinship obligations; rather, the fish were taken directly by the merchants who, largely through paper transactions, 'bought' the fish in exchange for necessary staples such as flour, sugar, and tea, and the provision of fishing gear for the coming season (cf. Faris, 1972; Chiaramonte, 1970). Essential control of the means of production, then, was in the hands of those who "do not carry on the productive process themselves"; and the "constitution of society" was based on a routing of goods and services to a power centre from which they were later re-directed (Wolf, 1966:3). This attempt to convert fluctuating and relatively low-priced fish into other staple commodities without supportive subsistence activities, such as gardening, made them extremely vulnerable to swings in world cod stocks and market prices, and earned for the people of this shore the appellation "slaves."

In 1929, this adaptation was disrupted by two successive catastrophes:

the crisis in international trade collapsed fish prices and left many families destitute, and later three tidal waves destroyed houses and fishing gear in the settlements, and disturbed the cod feeding grounds. For four years the cod virtually disappeared, and St. Lawrence and Lawn were forced to turn *en masse* to government relief.

In 1933, however, a private company began to exploit the fluorspar veins in the St. Lawrence area. Most of the men gave up fishing altogether, or undertook a new seasonal cycle: fishing in the summer and mining in the winter. Whichever option was taken, the men eventually left their traditional peasant economy for the world of industrial wage labour. But as we shall see, the break with their peasant past was only partial, and a measure of their traditionalist world view survived unscathed into the 1970s.

The transformation of St. Lawrence was more than economic. As early as the 1940s, not ten years after the opening of the mines, the men began to develop breathing difficulties. A pattern of early deaths followed soon after – from cancer caused by intensive radiation in the mines, and from silicosis and chronic obstructive pulmonary disease contacted from the atmosphere in the mines. Early attempts by concerned miners to establish the relationships between work in the mines and the diseases which were incapacitating or killing the miners were not encouraged by government or medical officials, an omission which caused great bitterness in the ravaged communities. In 1969, however, a Royal Commission finally established cause and effect, and recommended that a substantial number of disabled miners and widows receive Workmen's Compensation pensions.

By the time of writing, an estimated one hundred and fifty miners were dead and another hundred disabled[2] through industrial disease. In 1975, eighty-one widows were receiving widows' pensions from the Workmen's Compensation Board, and seventy-four disabled miners were receiving WCB pensions for industrial disease. Although the new Conservative Government has introduced a series of amendments to the Compensation Act designed to bring more families under the terms of the Act, a large number of miners and widows still feel they are under-compensated (and some are not compensated at all). Despite the humanitarian intent of the new government's amendments to the Act, profound bitterness still exists as a result of the WCB's activities in St. Lawrence and Lawn.

The paradox, more apparent than real, lies in the fact that the bureaucratic attempt to ameliorate the condition of St. Lawrence miners has created an additional spectrum of anxiety – for the WCB's acceleration of its relief to suffering workers brought with it as much mental despair as financial relief. The reason for this stems from the clash between bureaucratic and traditionalist cosmologies; for pensions which are awarded according to the impersonal and 'rational' criteria of the bureaucracy are seen by the traditionalist miners as awarded according to totally irrational and arbitrary criteria. Different pensions are given to individuals according to medical and bureaucratic criteria which make perfect sense in the Board rooms of St. John's, but which are utterly incomprehensible in traditionalist St. Lawrence and Lawn. Thus one miner is medically classified "30 percent disabled," and another "100 percent," and their pensions are calculated accordingly. But in the eyes of St. Lawrence and Lawn, these miners have all suffered from an identical trauma, "the mine disease." Moreover, only economic-functional classifications make sense to them: "You're either disabled or you're not." And the WCB's decisions to pay one miner, who can work, a substantial pension while they pay another miner who cannot work a tiny pension create extremely divisive forces within the communities. Similarly, one widow may receive a very large sum, whereas another may have her minute stipend cut off entirely.

These sources of perceived inequality create a social situation in which every person feels he or she is being treated unfairly, and the almost infinite gradations of disability classification and amount of pension create a correspondingly vast universe of discord. In the words of one elderly disabled miner, "it's all begrudgement nowadays." A bitterness and distrust pervade village affairs, and persuade the dying that the world has gone mad, filling their last remaining years with anxiety, confusion, humiliation, and doubt.

From the community's perspective, miners who have received an initial negative medical diagnosis must suffer not only the torment of their coming physical ordeal, but prepare for "the battle" for compensation. Now begins, what for them is, the process of begging for compensation and humiliating themselves before the doctors and the Compensation Board to show how sick they are. Once a miner is diagnosed as ill, and is "turned down" from employment in the mine, showing how sick he is becomes vital since the WCB is his only source of a "respectable" income. Once turned down by the mine, he has little chance of obtaining alternative employment as there are few employers in the area. More important, if he cannot obtain a 100-percent disability rating from the WCB, with the corresponding full pension, he is then "thrown over to welfare" and his income is determined by the infinitely less generous provisions of the Department of Social Assistance. Whereas '100 percenters' receive $225 per month plus $50 for each child in school, all ratings less than 100 percent are calculated according to a completely different formula which yields only a small pension, the sum of which is then deducted from the welfare cheque. Thus a miner with eight children and a 100-percent disability rating will receive $625 per month from the WCB, whereas if he had a 90-percent rating (or less), his income would be restricted to Welfare's $361 per month. Those who are denied a full disability pension not only suffer the loss of status implicit in accepting welfare, but they also suffer a near 50-percent reduction in income. It is these social and economic facts which provide the background to the battle with the WCB.

The Workmen's Compensation Board
The principle of workmen's compensation was established in the western industrial world in 1884, when Germany's compensation laws were first put into operation. Elsewhere, intense struggles ensued between spokesmen for industry and social reformers. Industry consistently challenged the logic and practicability of such legislation, arguing that it "was economically unsound and would shake the industries of Europe to their foundations" (F. I. McCanna in Royal Commission, 1969). Not until it was made clear that the *principle* of compensation removed responsibility for misadventure from the employer (that is, replaced individual employer's liability with collective liability), and that the *cost* of compensation could be spread and "figured in the cost of production, the same as depreciation in buildings, machinery, tools and other personal property employed in the process of manufacture" (*ibid.*) was compensation legislation accepted by the industrial world. By the time of the Great War, most industrial powers relented to the inevitable and framed compensation legislation.

Although compensation was introduced to Canada in 1910, there was no comparable move in Newfoundland until union with Canada in 1949; and the Newfoundland Workmen's Compensation Act did not come into effect until 1951. Prior to 1951, compensation was handled by private insurance companies for some industries, and by individual litigation by the worker against his employer in others.

Today, the WCB of Newfoundland and Labrador is a major bureaucratic structure employing sixty-eight persons; in 1974, 17,490 disease and accident claims were processed. WCB officials sometimes state that their ultimate goals are industrial safety and the "rehabilitation, retraining, and re-employment" of injured workers; in practice, however, less than 0.5 percent of their annual budget is spent on rehabilitation, and 1.9 percent on accident prevention. In 1974, the WCB's total expenditures were $7,999,958.77, and the book value of their long-term investments was $23,257,291.34 (WCB Annual Report: 6 ff). Total revenue for 1974, including assessments on both industry and investment income was $8,808,283.78. In 1974, the WCB was paying permanent pensions to 627 workmen (83 from the St. Lawrence disaster) wholly or partially disabled for life, and 302 widows (99 of whose husbands died from disease and accident in the St. Lawrence mines). The WCB attributes their lack of success in the area of rehabilitation to "the reluctance on the part of many employers to re-employ injured workmen in cases where permanent partial disability results from the accident," and observes that "this has a most demoralizing effect on injured workmen to the extent that many of them develop neuroses which are extremely difficult to combat'' (Annual Report, p. 9). As of 1975, no St. Lawrence miner disabled by industrial disease had requested or received WCB rehabilitation; yet according to the union, more than one out of two miners were injured in accidents in 1974.

In practice then, the WCB's efforts are focused almost exclusively on *indemnification* of injured workers, on the provision of "recompense to the workman for wage loss due to disability from personal injury by accident arising out of employment'' (Annual Report, p. 2). The hope of the social reformers who campaigned for compensation in the previous century was that it would create a "more friendly spirit" in industry by eliminating the "antagonism between the employee and employer engendered through accident litigation" (McCanna in Royal Commission, 1969) whereas in practice, it has merely removed the employer from the struggle, and moved the arena of conflict from the courts to the WCB. Although it has spared the worker the often ruinous expense of litigation in court and guaranteed him a measure of recompense, it has not removed him from the anxiety of the long battle with the WCB or from the social fact that he is subject to an institution whose behaviour he does not understand.

The WCB itself occupies an ambiguous position in society, as previously stated. WCB officials also express ambivalence in a number of spheres. An important one is the protection of industry versus the protection of workers. The dilemma is usually resolved, however, by the commonly heard justification, "After all, it's industry we have to answer to." Another area which could cause ambivalent feelings centres on whether their ultimate responsibilities are for indemnification of the injured worker or his rehabilitation into society. The officials explain their almost exclusive concentration on the former in terms of the economic impossibility of true rehabilitation in a depressed economy. A third dilemma is expressed as a moral one: where should the line be drawn between maximizing the returns to injured workers and eliminating the work ethic entirely? These issues are not unilaterally resolved for WCB officials, and the ambiguity introduces a sense of uncertainty into both long-term policy considerations and immediate decisions. Additionally, the division of responsibility between government, industry, and injured workmen exacerbates the 'delicacy' of or public sensitivity to WCB operations. This is reflected in the intense and often contradictory pressures besieging the WCB from the public, media, unions, individual workers, government, industry, and industry's lobbyists such as the Canadian Manufacturers Association Inc.

Although these ambiguities and countervailing pressures are important forces in limiting the ability of the WCB to accomplish its objectives, my concern is with the way the structure of regulations and the dissonance between two cosmologies make it impossible for the WCB to indemnify workers in St. Lawrence without leaving a train of ruinous social costs in the devastated communities. My responsibility in the remainder of this essay, then, is to show 'chapter and verse' how an efficient and 'rational' bureaucracy, staffed by officers of high quality, whose sole intent is to indemnify workers, whose instructions are to give all workmen the benefit of any doubt, nevertheless succeeds in adding to the bubbling pot of anguish as much as it removes.

If the explication of this paradox is our mandate, it is obviously a matter of more than academic concern: the devastated communities of St. Lawrence and Lawn live under conditions which are often financially intolerable and almost invariably socially destructive. The staff of the WCB, for their part, must swim through an abrasive miasma of public and private pressures, knowing all the while that their actions will be consistently misunderstood, their motives continually questioned, and their decisions almost universally reviled. I hope that the analysis which follows will be not only of interest to anthropologists concerned with the structure of bureaucracy, but of value to those who are charged with the responsibility of designing the major institutions in industrial society.

THE CLASH OF COSMOLOGIES

> "That crew in the Compensation building, there's fellows in there I'd love to hang" *Disabled Miner, August, 1974.*
> "They're all happy in St. Lawrence now. Yes, very happy" *WCB official, September, 1974.*

The Traditionalist Cosmology

St. Lawrence entered the second quarter of the 20th century as an essentially peasant society. Although its products were sold on world markets and subject to the vicissitudes of world economies, it was an isolated and traditional society whose "social equilibrium depended ... on a balance of transfers of peasant surpluses" to the merchants, and a reciprocal "provision of minimal security" to the fishermen (Wolf, 1973:279). Fishermen turned over their annual catches to merchants who in turn 'staked' them for their gear and household staples for the coming year. Whatever its feudalistic and paternalistic overtones, the system provided a measure of security for vulnerable and economically unspecialized communities that were isolated from the rest of the world and whose communal way of life was bound by tradition.

The introduction of wage labour with the establishment of the St. Lawrence Corporation's mining operation did far more than alter the work patterns of the people. The observation by Polanyi could be applied to St. Lawrence: "as the organization of labor is only another word for the forms of life of the common people ... the development of the market system would be accompanied by a change in the organization of society itself (1957:75)." St. Lawrence society was to become an accessory of a revised economic system. The wage economy "cut through the integument of custom, severing people from their accustomed social matrix in order to transform them into economic actors, independent of prior social commitments to kin and neighbors. They had to learn how to maximize returns and how to minimize expenditures, to buy cheap and to sell dear, regardless of social obligations and social costs" (Wolf, *ibid.*).

In St. Lawrence, the most profound consequence of this transformation was "their alienation from themselves to the extent to which they now had to look upon their own capabilities" not as personal characteristics in a personalized world, but as *marketable commodities*. Similarly they were alienated from their neighbours who had become "actual or potential competitors in the market" (Wolf, *op. cit.*:280), accelerating the centrifugal forces of household individualism which even before had curtailed community solidarity (cf. Chiaramonte, 1970). As elsewhere, "the fiction that men, land, and wealth were *nothing but* commodities entailed its own ruin" (Wolf, *ibid.*); the competition for jobs and status strengthened the indigenous forces of atomism in preparation for the final assault on *communitas* by the WCB.

Thus the men and women of St. Lawrence and Lawn, whose lives this essay touches, have in their own lifetimes passed through two major stages of economic and social history: from a traditional household-kin-community-centred existence to a capitalist wage economy in which their labour becomes a commodity and their neighbour a competitor. But the miners who have been stricken by one of the mine diseases have undergone a further socio-economic transformation. No longer able to market their labour, their *sole marketable commodity is now their disease*. Once classified as disabled and unable to find alternative work, their economic strategy must be to manipulate the benefits of the nation-state for their incomes. For the remainder of their days, the disabled miners' task is to exploit the diverse social agencies for whose benefits they are technically eligible – especially the WCB, but also the Department of Social Assistance (Welfare) and the Canada Pensions Plan.

They are singularly ill-equipped for such a task. If they have passed from peasants to wage labourers in their own lifetimes, if their social systems have been radically altered, the transformation is nonetheless imperfect and incomplete. If they are now subject to strengthened forces which spin apart kin and community, they nevertheless continue to perceive vast segments of social reality in a manner that is curiously unchanged. Still frequently illiterate and without access to education, in many ways they remain enmeshed in a traditionalist spiritual cosmology and a patronage polity regulated by the Roman Catholic Church and the provincial government, respectively. In such a traditionalist world, the disabled miner continues to perceive social relationships in personalistic terms and interprets action as a particularistic response to personal needs, and not in terms of the execution of formal regulations. And he continues to expect his patrons – the priest, the politician, the doctor, and the lawyer – to negotiate with the outside world on his behalf. Thus, even were he equipped with the educational tools necessary to comprehend the legalistic complexities of the Workmen's Compensation Act, the dictates of his traditionalist cosmology render incomprehensible the impersonal, formal, and universalistic criteria of bureaucratic legislation.

Thus it is that when a miner is "turned down,"[3] when his marketable commodity is transformed from his labour to his disease – with all the spiritual and social dislocations such a massive shift entails – his goal is to exploit the various public agencies to maximize his income. Because of the lack of coordination between these agencies, their relative value fluctuates over time: in the mid-1960s, welfare was often of greater value than workmen's compensation, but in the mid-'70s the disparity was reversed and disabled miners with large families could 'earn' almost double from compensation. Thus the failure of the disabled miner to 'sell' his disease effectively is a major financial blow; for as I have shown earlier, a maximally successful miner obtaining a 100-percent disability rating, and having six or eight children, can receive $625 compensation as against a maximum of $361 per month from welfare.

The *strategies* he employs in his attempt to maximize his returns are several, but they are consistently based on misperceptions of the compensation process. The most important strategy, as perceived by the disabled miner, is to use his patron-broker, the MHA (Member, House of Assembly). As elsewhere in Newfoundland, "the M.H.A. was expected by his constituent-clients to serve as both patron and broker," dispensing whatever "resources he himself controlled directly" and funnelling "requests from his constituents to the appropriate outside authority, agent, or institution," (Nemec, 1976:196). Although the patron-broker may have few first-order resources to distribute, he can demand that the WCB re-open a case or justify its previous negative decision. His demands, however, are relatively ineffective *vis-à-vis* the WCB. But in the eyes of the populace, the MHA's initiative is responsible for a positive decision, and in the case of a negative decision, even though his efforts have been unsuccessful, he continues "to work on it." In either case, the patron-broker consolidates his own position without necessarily and significantly altering the WCB decision.

The disabled miner's second major strategy, equally ineffectual, is to "keep after the Compensation," to be in continual contact in person and by mail until a satisfactory decision is reached, or until he accepts the impossibility of obtaining his "entitlement." The community's acceptance of this strategy is constantly bolstered by a misperception of the compensation process; for when a government legislative change in the Workmen's Compensation Act brings a new category of disease under the terms of the Act, the individuals affected by it assume that it is not a legislative change but the relenting by the WCB in their *particular* case because of their personal pressure on the Board.

Finally, the miner tries to make use of the local doctor. He thinks that by convincing him that his disease is sufficiently serious, the WCB doctors in St. John's will also be convinced and grant him a 100-percent disability rating. The local doctor, in fact, has relatively little influence over WCB medical decisions. Here, both doctor and miner are placed in untenable positions: in order for the doctor to avoid intolerable pressures he must dissociate himself from the task of influencing WCB decisions; and in order for the miner to live in the community as a man worthy of respect, he must minimize his symptoms and behave stoically in public while maximizing his symptoms to the local doctor. In both cases he relays essentially false information to the local doctor.

It should be obvious to the reader why I am not at liberty to discuss the ethnographic details of the miners' various strategies; but suffice it to say that *in each case* the miners misperceive the process by which they receive or are refused compensation. Their perception of the process is illustrated in the following account (edited and abridged) by a 52-year-old miner with lung cancer, now receiving a full pension.

"I got cancer of the left lung. I was going out to the barn and before I got out, I just held on to the barn, there was *that* much pain. So I came in and I said to me son, 'I don't think I'm going in to work this morning, I got to see the doctor, I got a hell of a pain.' The very minute the doctor seen me, he put me in the hospital right away. I thought I was having a heart attack. He told me then, he said, 'no, it's not a heart attack, but it's the next thing to it.' When I came out of hospital he warned me not to walk anywhere without using those pills. I can only move around quarter speed. I'm still holding me own. Cancer is not a thing that kills you overnight. Cancer is a thing that got to grow to do it. I mean I'll maybe go two, three years, perhaps five years. It just depends on how fast that's going to grow before it's going to kill you.

Now you asked me what the mine did for the people. This mine took *more* effect on the people of St. Lawrence and the people of Lawn and Lewin's Cove – those are the men got hurt by the mine. And they're in the graveyard, biggest kind of men too. Everyone my age, their fathers is gone; and everyone of my generation is on their way out. Now when I was a boy and this was a fishing town, wherever you'd go you'd see an old man then. It was all old men. The only thing we got out of this was a good big fat graveyard.

They'll send you in to St. John's to see a doctor. The first doctor they sent me in to, he took X-Rays because I wouldn't have no operation. Then they'll send you to the Compensation doctors, that's two fellows then you'll have to see. That's not all at one try now, that'll be the second time they send you in.

Then you got to start in. In order to get your compensation, you got to get ahold of your Member, and you got to get ahold of everybody that you know can try to get it for you. They don't want to give it to you *any* way. They just try to keep it. And they'll try every way, in every shape and form, to keep it away from you.

I was a twelve-month before I got it. You start to fight, trying to get your compensation then, and you got every doctor down there against you. They try to tell you you got TB, you got pneumonia, and you got this and you got something else. They knows goddam well what you got! Because it's only putting the 'scope on your chest and they can tell you.

I had to get ahold to our Member then, and I got him to work on it. In the last of it then, I got ahold to a lawyer, I wrote him and got him into it. And when they came to open that building up here (Recreation Centre), my son talked to our Member and this lawyer what worked to get the Special Fund for the widows and the people of St. Lawrence. So he had a talk with the two of them, and they opened that up there that night. He had a lot on his chest to get off, but he didn't get it all off that night because every now and then someone was coming in and they were shaking hands and what not, and he couldn't get the whole thing right across to them. But he got a lot of it across.

One of them guys said to him, had face enough to say to him, 'Do you think your father is eligible for compensation?' That made him mad, you know. 'Lord Jesus son,' he said, 'do you mean to tell me my father worked twenty years underground and is not eligible for compensation? Now look, if you're going to be talking, talk sense.' 'Well I don't know,' he said, 'you're right.'

But now this is how hard you got to work to get your compensation. That's a fact. And after I was off for a twelve-month, I got my compensation. I'm not saying I got any education, because I got none. But I got a lot of guts. That's one thing I always had. And I don't care who he is or where he comes from: he doesn't frighten me, and I'll stand up and talk to him as a man. I had to do it with all them fellows, the whole lot of them. But it took *me* a twelve-month to get my compensation. Fighting for it, and my wife – she was a school teacher – writing everybody that had anything to do with this, in order for me to get it then. And it took me a twelve-month before I got it.

We got a lot of sick miners here that's not getting it because the poor buggers couldn't fight their own battle. And they couldn't write on their own properly, and there was nobody. There was one woman up the lane here, her husband died just when I was starting work. She had seven or eight kids then, and she was on welfare – they didn't get no compensation then, that wasn't brought in till '51 – for ten or twelve years. When she got her compensation for her husband, they turned around and took the welfare out of it – they took that away from her! They were after turning around and taking away from her the welfare she raised her kids on. Fourteen or thirteen thousand. Now that's a fact.

But that's what you got to do in order to get it. You got to fight everyone right down to the bitter end in order to get anything out. If you don't do that, you don't get it. That's what you end up with, 'you can die if you like.'

I'm going to tell you something else. When they started me off on compensation and me Special Fund, they started me off on the Special Fund at the end of the year. They owed me 500 bucks, you see. They started me off on that month, when I'd been off work for a year: they should have started me off from the time I got sick, eh? They didn't give it to me at all. Now I don't know too much about that. So there's a guy that told me about it one day, he asked me one day I was in to the hospital there, and he was asking me if I got me Special Fund back from the time that I got sick or from the time I got my compensation. I said 'No, I got it from the time I got me Compensation, the time that I applied for it' – that was a year after I was off. 'Then I got it then. They sent me 50 bucks right from then on.' 'Well boy,' he said, 'there's a lot of fellows should have got that right from the beginning.' 'Well, by God,' I said, 'they're not going to get away with that from me then. If they owe me 500 bucks, I'm going to have it.' I went over and I got ahold of the union, and they got ahold of a man in St. John's, and I got my 500 bucks back.

Now who kept that back from me down there? Now somebody's crooked somewhere, I don't give a goddam who they are, somebody's got to be crooked, because they knew what time I came off work, and they knew that I should have got that money. That money was due me, eh!''

It is the source, variation, and consequence of this incomprehensibility and mistrust between bureaucratic and traditionalist cosmologies that is the focus of this essay.

The Bureaucratic Cosmology
WCB officials are often astonished and hurt to learn of the reactions of disabled workers and their families to Board decisions, for the officials do not see themselves as locked in battle with the people. To the contrary, they regard themselves as professionals and public servants, dispassionately administering government regulations on behalf of injured workmen. Moreover, they see their deliberations as not only dispassionate in quality,

but humanitarian in consequence: WCB total disability pensions, they say, are always equal to comparable benefits from the Department of Social Assistance, and are normally higher; WCB decisions are invariably loaded in favour of the workers, since government regulations specifically state that in questionable cases, "benefit of the doubt" should always be rendered to the workman.

WCB officials recognize that because of the delicate position they occupy in society, they are under constant and unjustified critical pressure. They often react with a sense of bewilderment to the workers' distrust of the WCB. Officials recognize that much of the criticism comes from the fact that workers cannot understand WCB regulations, and they respond by providing illustrations from other bureaucratic sectors in their own lives in which they are in "similar" positions: "I don't understand insurance regulations, but I trust my insurance man to do the right thing. Why can't they trust us?"

One incident which occurred during my fieldwork was much discussed as an illustration of this lack of understanding and trust. Six months previously, a sixty-four year-old man had been awarded a partial disability pension of $79.00 per month. He came to the Board in a rage, demanding to know how they expected him to live on $79.00 a month. The WCB protested that government regulations did not allow them to support partial disability claimants, and the WCB was charged only with the responsibility of compensating him for a specific injury; under the Terms of the Act, this amount was all they could offer him. When the worker insisted that something be done because his age rendered him unemployable, the Board suggested that his pension be renegotiated to dovetail with Old Age Pension benefits for which he would be eligible in six months' time. The WCB suggested that they raise the worker's WCB pension to $225 per month until he became eligible for the Old Age Pension of $200 per month. At that time, the WCB pension would be reduced to the old rate minus the repayment of the advance; that is, between the WCB and the Old Age Pensions, the worker would have a minimum of $225 a month for the rest of his life.

"This was explained several times to the worker to make sure that he understood," said a WCB official. In November, 1975, when the worker turned sixty-five, the WCB accordingly reduced his WCB pension to the agreed amount. The worker was outraged and came into the WCB demanding to see the chairman. Brandishing letters from the Prime Minister of Canada, his MHA, and his lawyer, all of whom stated that "there is no connection between Old Age Pensions and the Workmen's Compensation Board" (a statement which the worker took to be official rejection of the WCB's right to dovetail the two pensions), the worker insisted that the Board "had guaranteed him the $225 a month for the rest of his life" without reference to anything else. Such incidents, willful or not, descend upon the officials and often convince them that communication with the public is impossible, that they are doomed to be forever slandered.

The particular ideology which provides moral imperatives and constrains action on the part of the WCB officials is a distinctive blend of a rigidly codified set of regulations (the Workmen's Compensation Act and its many amendments), of a recognition of the financial responsibility of the WCB to industry, of an uncoordinated melange of philosophical and political ideas garnered during the lifetime of the officials, and of the morals learned from the exchange of difficult or illustrative cases between officials. The WCB bureaucrat learns these ideological constraints in no particularly programmed fashion; rather, he brings with him to the WCB his personal ideas, reads the Act until its stipulations are clear to him, and then absorbs as much as he can of WCB philosophy and case histories as he moves through the organization.

The ultimate source of ideological constraint is the Workmen's Compensation Act of 1951 – its 106 sections, and its many amendments. A highly abridged summary of the Act and its amendments follows, focusing only on the issues important to St. Lawrence.

1951: The WC Act came into effect, providing compensation only for accidents and silicosis.

1960: An amendment to the Act provided compensation for lung cancer arising from underground work.

1972: Chronic obstructive pulmonary disease (hereafter referred to as COPD) was brought under the terms of the Act, and miners named by the Royal Commission Report as being entitled were compensated.

1973: Surface workers as well as underground workers were compensated; earlier restrictions, requiring men to work underground (between 1951 and 1960), were eliminated; and benefits were increased to the extent that a miner would not be paid less than his widow.

1975: Compensable diseases extended to include any cancer possibly related to mine employment.

Thus the purpose of each change since 1951 has been either to bring under the terms of the Act a new class of disabled workers by compensating additional diseases or category of workers, or to increase the amount of the pensions paid to the disabled miners.[4] With respect to codified government legislation, WCB officials have no alternative but to follow its instructions. But where cases are not clear-cut and where mechanical decisions are impossible, the ideological sources beyond the Act are of some significance in WCB operations, especially in areas where they are given discretionary powers.

Although WCB officials regard themselves as rational and impartial public servants, dispassionately carrying out the dictates of the Act, the total financial dependence of the WCB upon industry creates a convergence of class interests which is reflected in officials' philosophies. This is particularly evident among members of the Board whose pride in the WCB is expressed in terms of its financial reputability – "this is an $8,000,000-a-year operation, one of the soundest in the province" – and who compare the substantial annual surplus of the Newfoundland WCB with others such as Nova Scotia's, "which squeaked through last year with less than a $100,000 surplus." Officials' identification with industry is justified not only in crude power terms but also in terms of a commitment to the importance of industry and its ethics – especially the work ethic. Thus WCB officials remind themselves that "we need industry," that the demands of unions "will wreck industry" and "drive industry out of the province." This identification is expressed in a consistent alignment of interest in opposition to workers' interests. Thus miners' union demands for the right of miners to refuse to enter a shaft they regard dangerous is discussed as an illustration of both the "lack of trust" of workers for management, and as a demand for principles which open the way to "terrible abuse": "the miner could just say that any place was dangerous he didn't feel like going to. An excuse to go home and watch TV."

A related constant concern to higher WCB officials is the erosion of "the work ethic" – perhaps the fundamental value of the WCB – and fear for any part which the WCB pensions might play in this erosion. Frequently cited research, conducted in the U.S., suggests that granting WCB pensions for more than a few months breaks the work habits of the workmen and makes them psychologically incapable of returning to work: indeed, specific statistical projections are referred to, which state that after one year of unemployment, 90 percent of workers are incapable of returning to their jobs. Familial roles become reversed, so that wives go to work while husbands tend the home. It is concluded that irreparable psychological damage is done to the recipient of compensation. These "data" permit philosophical stances which suggest that WCB pensions and benefits may do more harm than good and should therefore be restricted.

WCB officials receive no formal training in WCB philosophy, other than an intensive period of reading the Act; they also carry with them a 'grabbag' of perceptions and morals collected in the course of their varied lives. Although such perceptions might be challenged if they conflicted with the orientation of the Board, and a truly deviant individual might be removed from the organization, these ideas are not challenged if there is no fundamental contradiction with WCB interests. Officials' perceptions of the behaviour of the people of St. Lawrence and Lawn then vary from compassion and acuity of judgement based upon, what is essentially, an insightful amateur sociology, to an absence of insight and a concomitant exasperation, which takes on the following kinds of logic:

The people of the communities do not understand our regulations, yet they have no trust in us. They know everyone else's business, they know who got an increase, and they expect everyone to get an increase.
Often I think the money is no good for them, they don't know what to do with it and just throw it away, and then they complain that they don't get as much as the other person.
And they come here expecting you to do everything for them, such as a widow wanting her roof fixed. But we don't do that kind of thing, we pay compensation.
All they seem to think about is money.
Once I asked one of the widows, ''how much would you want? How much would be enough?'' They never know, they'll ask anything.

Although officials making such explicit statements are rare, the adversary relationship between workers and WCB clearly exacts its toll. Complaints are widespread about the ''lack of initiative'' and the apparent obsession of the communities with financial gain. Nor should it be surprising that individuals react in this manner, for WCB officials must continually bear the onslaught, often face-to-face, of insults and abuse from aggrieved workers or widows, and they are given no opportunity to see any other side of St. Lawrence and Lawn.

More important than personal philosophies in the formation of ideology and the patterning of decisions is what is learned through discussion of particular cases and philosophical stances. These discussions (largely informal 'coffee-table' talk) are meant to illustrate the finer points of WCB dilemmas and intentions, and they act as precedents in the 'court' of the WCB. They are thus part of the process of an attempt to establish a coherent WCB ideology. Here, ideological stances are made concrete through empirical illustration or abridged philosophies. Each case is a story with a moral and the moral provides the rationale for specific future decisions. The instances I discuss below are regarded as classic by WCB officials; they are freely communicated and shared throughout all levels of the hierarchy, and they impinge upon major areas of WCB activities.

1. Why miners, disabled by many diseases, were not compensated until political pressure was placed on the WCB in the 1970s.
   WCB officials are often bewildered by the incorporation of diseases under the Act which can be attributed to causes other than industry. Hence, they argue that St. Lawrence's damp and foggy climate would produce endemic COPD (especially chronic bronchitis and emphysema) even without the presence of a mine; that the traditional diet, high in calories and low in important nutrients, would contribute to a high rate of heart disease; and that the miners' heavy cigarette smoking would contribute to a high rate of lung cancer even without underground

radiation. WCB officials feel that legislation takes no account of "cause and effect" or of the normal occurrence of these diseases, and that people have been compensated for diseases which were not linked to industry; hence the cynicism implicit in the following remark: "Wait till the first female office worker in St. Lawrence develops cancer of the breast or cervix; we'll be expected to pay." The deduced moral behind these remarks is that the range of compensable diseases should be restricted to proven industrial links.

2. In Ontario, the WCB pays compensation for pain and discomfort whereas the Newfoundland WCB does not.

This is explained in terms of the impossibility of determining with scientific precision the degree of pain and discomfort a worker has suffered. "How can you really tell if he is in pain? Two men will have the same complaint, but one will say he's suffering terribly while the other won't even mention it. Some men will tell you they have been in constant pain for years, but any doctor will tell you that human beings can't be in constant pain, the human body can't take it, it's impossible."[5] Thus differences in individuals' pain thresholds and the possibility of malingering make scientific adjudication difficult or impossible. *Moral*: Therefore, no compensation should be provided for pain and discomfort.

3. Unforeseen unfortunate consequences of awarding a disability pension.

A 62-year-old worker strains his back lifting a twenty-pound object and is given full compensation benefits. The employer berates the WCB and swears he will never hire another elderly worker because his WCB assessment will now increase. *Moral*: Pensions should be curtailed.

4. The true wisdom of non-functional disability ratings.

These ratings sometimes appear to lack common sense; for example, an office worker who has lost both legs can receive a 100-percent life pension on the basis of his medical loss despite the fact that he could be back at work on full salary within six months, whereas a watch repairman who loses a few fingers receives only a small disability pension despite his being rendered unemployable. This may appear to be foolish, but the percentage ratings embodied in the International Table of Rates are "the results of years of experience by doctors all over the world," and represent a true picture of medical impairment. *Moral*: WCB disability ratings may appear to lack sense, but they are, in fact, based on precise and scientific calculations that are accepted internationally.

5. The logic of partial disability ratings.

Mr. C., a St. Lawrence ex-miner, is crippled with severe bronchitis and heart disease and there is no doubt that he is permanently and totally disabled. Yet he receives only a 60-percent disability rating and a correspondingly small pension, which is deducted from his welfare payments. But he is categorized as 60-percent-disabled because the medical team whose job "is to establish cause and effect deduces that Mr. C.'s heart disease is a result of childhood rheumatic fever, and not of industry. Therefore, only 60 percent of his total disability can reasonably be attributed to industrial exposure." *Moral*: Although the workers may not understand it, the system of disability ratings is "scientific" and makes sense.

6. The logic behind the WCB's incomplete coverage of industry.

   Some groups are exluded from WCB coverage because they are unable to pay their own way. For example, a contractor hires a man to put shingles on the roof of one house. His payments to the WCB total only ten or fifteen dollars. One day, the worker might fall off the roof and be killed; then the WCB would have to pay his widow thousands of dollars in pension – "that'd be alright for the widow, I suppose, but very hard on the Board." Additionally, a lot of smaller companies are 'fly-by-nighters,' such as taxi firms, and it would be a terrible job administering them. To prevent this indemnity from occurring, the WCB does not cover some small industries. *Moral*: Lack of WCB coverage for all workers is justifiable.

7. The rationale for the WCB's reluctance to commute pensions and pay lump sums instead.

   The argument is approximately the following: if you give most workers a large lump sum, they just go out and blow the whole thing. Or they invest it in an unrealistic business venture, like chip vans and grocery stores, and go bankrupt. We have a responsibility to the worker and to ourselves: A few years later, he may meet someone and say: "yes I've lost a leg and I'm getting no compensation." And he's not lying. Besides, the commutation of pensions disrupts our investment sequence, since our administrative costs are almost equal to our investment income from pension reserves. *Moral*: Granting lump sums has undesirable effects on both worker and WCB, and should be avoided.

8. The impossibility of a rehabilitation programme in an underdeveloped economy.

   The excellent programme operated, for example, by Alberta's WCB, in which disabled workers are put on full compensation while being retrained and then placed in a new job, would not be possible in Newfoundland because there are no jobs to put them in. The poor-cousin situation of Newfoundland as a "hewer of wood and drawer of water for Ontario," with no secondary industry to absorb retrained injured workers, makes serious rehabilitation impossible. *Moral*: The WCB's low effort in rehabilitation is justified in Newfoundland.

9. Unintended consequences of WCB procedures.
One worker came to the WCB to accelerate the processing of his claim in a state of extreme tension. His heart disease, while real, could not be related to industry, and a tentative decision was made to deny him compensation. On the return drive home, he had a heart attack and died soon after. WCB doctors said it was possible the trauma of his ordeal with the bureaucracy contributed to his heart attack, and the decision was therefore reversed in his favour "without going into the technicalities of the case," so that his widow received a full pension. *Moral*: Compassion is our guiding principle.

In sum, although WCB officials rarely understand the traditionalist cosmology of St. Lawrence (and vice versa), they are often aware of some of the contradictions and paradoxes in WCB legislation and operations. However, their bureaucratic ideology – a combination of government legislation, class identity, personal background, and WCB case experience – limits both comprehension and resolution of critical contradictions.

CONTRADICTIONS OF LOGICAL MODE

So far I have sketched the parameters of what appear to be two very different ideological systems. A traditionalist defines social relationships in personalistic terms and expects decisions to be informed by individual and informal qualities. He perceives the bureaucrats' behaviour in terms of three negative qualities: *irrationality* (no cause and effect relationship is understood in WCB decisions); *unfairness* (some are rewarded whereas others in the same position are deprived); and *arbitrariness* (no comprehensible reason exists for rewarding some and punishing others). On the other hand, a bureaucrat defines social behaviour in universalistic and formal terms, and is required to make decisions based on an impersonal administration of codified regulations. He perceives the traditionalists' behaviour in terms of three negative qualities also: *ignorance* of WCB regulations, an apparent *obsession* with material gain, and a *refusal* to accept the impartiality of regulations.

In fact, however, there is considerable ideological congruence between the cosmologies. Both 'sides' begin with a variation of the same principle – that all men should be treated equally. What varies is the way they perceive equality of treatment and the conclusions they draw from these different constructions. The traditionalists believe that each individual has a right to be treated the same way by everyone; that miners' disabilities should be assessed by essentially economic criteria; and their conclusion is that all victims of "the mine disease" should receive a total disability rating. The bureaucrats mean by equality the principle of uniform scientific assessment: that all men should be assessed according to the same specific medical criteria; and their conclusion is that there are different degrees of impairment and disability.

What happens then is that each side uses different criteria to evaluate disability and to construct typologies of similarity and dissimilarity. Traditionalist logic is based on the following reasoning:
(1) those miners who are sick have the mine disease;
(2) those with the mine disease are economically disabled;
(3) those who are so disabled should receive full pensions as compensations, as should their widows. Bureaucratic logic takes an alternative sequence:
(1) only some miners have one of the scheduled industrial diseases (cancer, silicosis, COPD);
(2) their diseases vary in degree of severity;
(3) they should be compensated according to the degree of their medical impairment and not according to their economic disability;
(4) widows should be pensioned only if the husband actually dies of one of the scheduled industrial diseases.
Thus, what varies are the typologies: bureaucratic classification of case types is determined on the basis of scientific cause and a medically demonstrated degree of impairment, whereas traditionalist criteria are based on the economic consequences of the diseases.

The ironic result of these alternative constructions is that each side sees itself as operating in terms of *universalistic* social principles; but, in fact, both sides accuse the other of violating the principle of egality by operating in *traditionalist* terms: the traditionalists accuse the bureaucrats of making their decisions on the basis of patronage, influence, and a desire to defraud the miners of their "just entitlement," and the bureaucrats see the traditionalists as using patronage and influence in their attempt to ride roughshod over universal principles and defraud the WCB of its funds.

I wish to examine some of the critical contradictions which arise from the clash of these logical modes. In so doing, I must ask the reader to indulge the ethnographic detail, for individual, community, and bureaucratic perceptions must be catalogued and explicated. What follows is a sampling of what are regarded as WCB depredations by the people of St. Lawrence and Lawn, especially the disabled. Each item can be, and frequently is, pulled from their 'warehouse' to demonstrate the perfidy of the WCB and its arbitrary differential treatment of what they regard as identical cases. As such, each case provides lyric and note for the orchestration of their anguish.[6]

Case One: Two Widows
A. *Traditionalist perception.* Two widows whose husbands died of

"the miner's disease" are treated completely differently: one receives a monthly widow's pension, whereas the other's compensation benefits have been cut off entirely. "I'll tell you now one case that's after happening here: a fellow's after dying, and he worked with me underground, George Molloy. He was sent into St. John's the early fall, and he got his compensation, he got $2800 backtime. I don't know what his monthly salary was, but according to what his lump sum was, it couldn't have been more than fifty, sixty dollars a month. And as soon as he died, they cut his wife off right away. She never got a cent since. I don't know how that happened, because there's another woman over there, her husband died and she still gets it" (Lawn miner, 1974).

b. *Widow's perception.* "He started (mining) because he never made anything that summer fishing, and there was nothing else left for him to do. He had to go in the mine. He grabbed whatever there was. He was the first man (from Lawn) to go into the mine, that was in '42 or '43. The last time he was there was '51: they had to take him out of the mine with this stuff that was on his chest. It must have been silicosis, because how did he get the compensation to give him, eh? He got a bit of money last year, whenever they started to give it out last year, see, a year ago. Tell you what he got, $2,700 he got, and $75 a month. Then when he died they cut it off. They took it away then after he died. They never give me nothing. The death certificate, it said something about the lung, and the liver, and the pancreas."

"But the most of them that died here, they just kept them on that. I mean, certain women here that their husbands died – some died with heart trouble really, and more of them died with suffering on the chest – and they still got it after their husbands died. There's only me and another woman that's after being like this and can't get it. That Hallinan man that died in June, she was cut off too as soon as he died, and he was getting compensation."

"Yes, that's right. Some people is getting it and more is not. No, I can't understand it either. I can't see why it happened. Their children get so much a month, and the allotment still come to their wife. I don't understand it – there's five or six women here in this harbour like that. I wrote to Dr. Pittman (WCB official) and he always sends back and says I'm not entitled to it. So that's it. I didn't bother no more then" (Mrs. George Molloy, Lawn widow, 1974).

c. *Bureaucratic perception.*[7] Mr. Molloy's claim was "accepted for 30 percent disability as from 1 September, 1969. Our Act of 1972 would not permit us to go back beyond that date" in calculating back-time payments. "It is to be noted that Mr. Molloy's disability from respiratory disease was considered to be mild and that he suffered from other things such as heart disease, gastro-intestinal disease, and carcinoma of the head of the pancreas which were not compensable under the Act at the time. Mr. Molloy died on 18 December, 1973 of carcinoma at the head of the pancreas and we had no alternative but to stop payments at that time because this cause of death was not compensable.'' (With the 1975 Amendment, however, many cancers became compensable.) ''We have now accepted the claim for death benefits as from date of death.''

Those widows who did continue to receive benefits did so if their husband's cause of death fell under the terms of the Act. Thus Mrs. Rebecca Flynn, whose husband died of silicosis in 1964, ''was immediately placed in widow's benefits which she is now receiving at the rate of $225 per month.''

D. *Comment.* The clash of cosmologies and the lack of mutual comprehension of their associated logical modes are elegantly summarized by the participants in the above case. From the point of view of the traditionalist widow and community, Mr. Molloy received a savagely low disability rating and pension for a man disabled by ''the miner's disease,'' when he had worked as hard and as long as the other miners who received 100-percent disability pensions. Then, when he died of ''the miner's disease'' his widow's payments were unjustly cut off. According to the bureaucratic cosmology, however, Mr. Molloy's case was processed strictly according to government regulations, and the characteristics of his case were entirely different from the other miners: only 30 percent of his disability could be related to industrial causes (the remainder were 'natural'), and he died of a type of carcinoma which was not compensable at the time of his death.

These disparities between cosmologies generate the intellectual dissonace between traditionalists and bureaucrats, and the bewilderment which characterizes relations between the communities and the WCB. The Lawn community could not see why the widow was denied compensation after her husband's death, since he was receiving it before he died. Was this not proof that the WCB accepted the cause of his death as mine-linked? How could the WCB suddenly behave as if he did not have the mine disease? The WCB in turn was frustrated by the widow's incomprehension of their own distinctions: was it not clear that although Mr. Molloy suffered from a compensable disease, he died of another? Regardless, their decision was determined by law.

Case Two: Two ''Blinded'' Miners

A. *Traditionalist perception.* In this case, two men who each lost an eye in mine accidents received completely different treatment from the WCB. One received a large lump sum enabling him to start a business, whereas the other received only a tiny pension of twenty-two dollars per month even though he was almost totally unable to earn a living.

B. *Miner's perception.* ''The way it actually happened was that I was looking up the shaft, a small piece of rock came down and busted the eye.

That was in 1956. I was eighteen. It was bleeding a nice bit. First when it happened now I didn't think it was the eye was busted. I got to the hospital and they stitched up the eye and they left me there then for two weeks and three days. Then they transferred me from that to St. John's on a boat – that was in the wintertime see, and mostly the roads were blocked. So it took us just about two days to make the trip to St. John's: we used to go so far, then stay overnight, then go the rest of the way afterwards.''

"First thing we had to do was look for a boarding house. They didn't put me in the hospital right away. I had both eyes covered, and mother was with me at the time, she was leading me just the same as a blind man. I was there 'round a week before they operated on the eye. They brought in all kinds of specialists to see if the eye could be saved, but they told me they left me in St. Lawrence too long. If they had sent me on straight from the mine the eye could have been saved, but it was too far gone then and all the nerves were gone. They told me if they left the eye the way it was, it would only interfere with the other one, so I told them go ahead and take it out. And that's what they did. I only got the one eye now and I got to try to look after that.''

"I got compensation right away. I started off at twenty-two dollars a month. But I came back to the same company looking for a job on the surface, and the boss asked me what kind of work I could do. I told him I could drive a truck. And he said, ''*Well*, you can drive a truck. Any two-year-old youngster can come in and tell me that.'' That's the satisfaction I got from them. They wouldn't take me back on the job anymore. They told me they had nothing for me to do. That was it for the company, and I never got an offer of work from them after.''

"The company don't exist anymore anyway, that was the St. Lawrence Corporation. The Rehabilitation Officer at the Workmen's Compensation, he tried everything possible to get work for me there, but he said it was like fighting a brick wall. Then the big thing came up, the medical. You had to have a medical for any job you went on. Once that turned up I was finished. It I had to have a medical, I was turned down for any job.''

"Injured eye,'' that's what I'm classified as. After I got a lawyer on it, he raised it from $22.04 to $29.02. That lawyer, I'm not really exact whether it's 100 or 300 he charged that time. And then Eric Jones was our member (M.H.A.) at the time, and I got after him and he rose it from $29.02 to $46.78. That $70 that I'm getting now, that was automatically a raise from the Compensation itself; I never went after it.''

"It's a hard fit-out to try to figure out, the Compensation, You can't figure them out. After I came home from the hospital, I started off to try to find out how to get some money for it. I got ahold to a man in St. Lawrence, he worked for the same company, he lost the same eye, and he done okay. But he wouldn't put on to me how he come round to getting it. I went to him and found him in his own front room and asked him how he come to get on the pad, get some money, and the only words he told me was, ''I worked for it.'' That's the satisfaction I got from him. He said, ''All I can tell you is I worked for it.'' But he did okay because he got a lump sum, I don't know how much, but they started him up in a meat market, bought him a truck – I think it was the Compensation. He got a lump sum before that, but I don't know how much; and they started him off at $120 a month. *And how come one man's eye is different than the other?* That's what I told the people when I was up before the Board, that I didn't think that was that much difference; mine was blue and his was brown. They just laughed it off. And I told them I knew he was getting that much, and they said no, they were paying him off because he fell down.''

''I filled out applications in the Board office for to take a course in vocational school in Burin, and I never heard tell of it afterwards. That's about six year ago. I would be still interested. I believe they told me they used to pay $90 a week while I was training. I was going to try to get back to them this year.''

''Then I was doing only just odd jobs here and there. I had to visit the Welfare Officer. Some think it's an awful thing: it's something I wouldn't go for unless I was really drove to. I don't know if everyone feels the same as I do, but I don't feel one bit comfortable at it. It's like you can't go meet someone face to face, you're always keeping clear. Some officers are half decent fellows, and you'll meet some damned hard fellows. Some will meet you half way and some more, it's like they're paying out of their own pockets. Sometimes they do have a queer thing to say; they got the idea that you're not looking for employment, you're only just sponging off them.''

''What I see right now, five years from now I'll be the same as what I am now. That's the only thing I can look forward to. Because if I've got to take another job anywhere else, there's a medical concerned, and I'm finished. When I was going back and forth to St. John's, visiting the Compensation to see what I could get from them, I took a course for a mechanic and I took a course for a mason. I did very good with each test, and they told me afterwards it wasn't such a good idea after all. Because they said for a mason, he could be eight or nine stories up and turn a blind side to the scaffold, and you're gone over. And a mechanic could be underneath a vehicle and it could fall down.''

''It started in '56 when I had the eye out. After that I had an operation for a stone in the kidney, and a prostrate gland removed. And then I had a ruptured appendix: both times I was took emergency from St. Lawrence to St. John's. Everyone else is doing good. The wife herself, she had a sickness for eight or nine year – miscarriages – and she had low blood. She always used to go into hospital and take blood. In 1972, I wasn't home to dinner and the young fellow told me the house was afire. It was freezing and the pumps on the fire truck used to freeze up, couldn't make any headway at it. And around twelve, she was flat.''

"If I go to bed now at bedtime, I won't go to sleep till about five, six o'clock in the morning. I don't know what's the cause of it. I can't get rest somehow. I think what started it was when the house burnt. You know, it keeps crossing me mind and you're not satisfied to go to sleep because you think any minute now she could go again. The least little crack you hear, you think it's a fire. I used to eat good too. Fellows I used to work with used to call me a garbage can, because whatever they had left they'd pass along and I ate it. It seems like I'm always hungry, but when I sit down to eat, I can't eat. It kind of wears you down after a while.''

c. *Bureaucratic perception*. "Mr. Duff was injured on 29 February, 1956 while looking up a shaft opening; he was struck by something, possibly ice, in the right eye. The eye was subsequently removed in March. He was originally awarded an 18-percent permanent partial disability pension for enucleation of the right eye. This gave him a monthly pension of $22.65, calculated according to his wages of $188.76 a month. However, on the basis of new evidence of his earnings, Mr. Duff's pension was increased to $29.04 a month. Following this, a report was received that he had poor vision in his left eye (not in any way related to the accident) which was corrected somewhat with glasses. In June, 1957, the Board noted this condition and felt that a larger permanent partial disability pension would be warranted, and that the claim would be reviewed when the Board clarified its eye disability assessment situation. This was done in April, 1958, and Mr. Duff's disability award was increased by 11 to 29 percent. This brought his monthly pension to $46.78 retroactively effective from May, 1956. Subsequent amendments to the Act have increased his pension to the current rate of $87.00 a month.''

"There is nothing to stop anybody from making representation on behalf of an injured workman, including himself. This is good, for it might bring something to the attention of the Board which might otherwise be overlooked. However, the present Board makes its decisions based on facts as they see them and will not be pressured into decisions which are not compatible with the Act or its intentions. Mr. Eric Jones, M.H.A. for Burin, did make representation on Mr. Duff's behalf in 1958, but as indicated above, the Board had decided in June, 1957 to review Mr. Duff's claim and award him a larger percentage disability award because of the poor vision in the eye which had not been injured. Representations are heeded, of course, but it matters not the source.''

"Mr. Sullivan's case [the other claimant referred to] is quite different from Mr. Duff's. He was subjected to a blast injury involving the whole of his face. He lost his left eye and his right eye was also severely injured; in fact with a vision of 20/80 which cannot be improved with glasses, he could be classified as nearly blind. Mr. Sullivan also suffers from silicosis and because of these several conditions, he is regarded as 100-percent-disabled.''

"In 1961, in an effort to rehabilitate himself, Mr. Sullivan requested 12 percent of his pension in a lump sum payment. This request was acceded to. However, subsequent events proved that this did not work out. [He had invested the sum in a small business which failed.] And unfortunately because of this his monthly pension payments are now based on an 88 percent disability even though he is totally disabled. There is no way to compare Mr. Duff's case with Mr. Sullivan's as they are completely different. The similarity begins and ends with the fact that they each had an eye enucleated. That was the total extent of Mr. Duff's injury, but Mr. Sullivan's severe injury to his other eye and his silicosis have produced a case of total disability.''

D. *Comment*. It should be clear that according to the WCB's bureaucratic criteria, the above two cases are completely different: Duff is 29-percent-disabled according to the International Standard Table of Rates, whereas Sullivan is totally disabled. These percentage classifications have no meaning in St. Lawrence. Yet because government regulations prohibit the WCB from economic/functional classifications of disability, the social fact that Duff is no longer able to ''earn a decent living'' and is *functionally* totally disabled is not allowed to enter the analysis.

Nor does the nature of the traditionalist communities permit a measure of reconciliation for Duff, since the atomisn inherent in the communal structure restricts the flow of information within the communities. As the communities are convinced that worker-WCB relations are a zero-sum game and the WCB a limited resource, like the fishery, in which one party can benefit only at the expense of another worker, Sullivan is virtually prohibited from explaining which 'techniques' he used to obtain his higher disability classification. For, implicit in the equation is the fear that he might endanger his own pension.

Regarding rehabilitation, WCB regulations specify that the initiative must come from the injured worker before the Rehabilitation Division can act; Duff, however, is waiting for them to approach him.

As in the other cases, although it is clear that the WCB has minutely and precisely administered the government regulations, the clash between the logical modes renders their decisions incomprehensible, and adds to the illustrative case load of perfidy in St. Lawrence.

Case Three: Arbitrary Decisions and Unnecessary Battles
A. *Traditionalist perception*. Jack Callaghan, a 51-year-old ex-miner, recently classified as 100-percent-disabled with silicosis, is seen as an illus-

tration of the arbitrariness of WCB decisions, now classifying a man as perfectly healthy, now as totally disabled; and of the artificial battle between community and Board begun without just cause and culminated without reason.

B. *Miner's perception.* "You had to go get a medical. So I went down to get a medical. A week was up and I had to go back for a report. So I gets in to the doctor and Jesus, he was frightened to death. I said, I'm supposed to get a medical to go to work. 'Lord,' he says, 'you're not going to work, you're going home.' Not too long after that I gets a call to go in to St. John's. So I went up to Dr. Wilder and he goes all over me and everything and tells me me chest is rotten, 'You have a cruel bad chest.' So he give me another paper and I had to go to the General Hospital for some more tests. The doctor he say he wanted an operation. So I told him, 'No, I'm not taking no operation.' I suppose they must have got fed up on me then, so they sent me home. They wouldn't give me the money, but it was a good spell before they bothered me anymore."

"In April they called me back to the Confederation Building. Three doctors there then. Lord Jesus, one fellow got me in there and he went all over me, twisting and turning and drawing. He went out and the other fellow come in, and he done the same. Then the other fellow come in and he done the same. If they hadn't knocked off I would have fallen on the floor because it was too much. I wasn't feeling that well, and they were forcing you."

"Put me clothes on and the doctor took me down to this great big board. 'There's your X-Ray,' he said, 'there's all evidence of silicosis there. But we got to have a piece of your lung to have the real proof.' 'You're not getting no piece of my lung,' I said. 'Well sir,' he said 'the proof is there, you got it; but we can't do nothing for you till we gets the real proof.' He wanted a piece. Dr. Wells there, he said, 'You know Mr. Callaghan, we got to have proof before we can give you Compensation.' I said, 'Well, you're not getting no piece of my lung! Everyone ye cut, do you know where they're at? They're in the graveyard.' But he said, 'Today we got all new equipment and everything, the latest.' I said, 'They're not made yet that's going to cut me.' He said, 'I'll tell you what we'll do. You go home; and if they takes the Social away from you, we'll give your compensation.' That's the words he said to me, so help me God! I knows men that worked there twenty years that they never give nothing to."

"They thought sure to get to operate on me. The Little Devil I called him, that was his name, Dr. Mack. He took me over to the board. That was very, very selfish for a man to take you over and show you your own disease. 'There it is,' he says, 'there's all evidence of silicosis. We got to have the real proof, a piece of your lung.' In the neck they cuts you and gets a piece of you. My son, anyone's got that and he takes the operation, just like that!

Not one of them lived. They could have said, 'Well boy, go on home, we'll send you your cheque.' What was mine was mine.''

"Whatever year I got it, I gets a call to go out to the Compensation Board. I was up before the Board so long. And all that doctor done with me the next morning; I went up and just hauled off me shirt, he went around me chest, and back and forth over my back, that was all. And two weeks after that I had me money, $6,700. And all before that they wanted to operate, operate.''

C. *Bureaucratic perception.* "There is no battle. Both the WCB and its staff do everything within the limitations of our legislation to ensure that workmen obtain the benefits to which they are entitled. The Board well understands the frustrations experienced by some St. Lawrence miners and their widows. It is difficult for claimants to understand the reason for some claims' being accepted while others were not. The Act provides compensation for some diseases but not for others. Silicosis was a compensable disease since the inception of the Board, but if the husband died of some other cause which was not compensable, it was difficult to make the widow understand why she did not continue to receive a pension.''

"Mr. Callaghan was diagnosed as having chronic pulmonary obstructive disease and September 1, 1969 was the first date this condition became compensable. His claim was accepted for 100-percent disability on that date" [under the terms of the 1972 Workmen's Compensation (Amendment) Act, Section 91B (3) and (4)].

D. *Comment.* This case demonstrates the mutual incompatibility of the two cosmologies and their logical modes. The community's ethnomedicine conceives of "the mine disease" as a single disability caused by both silicosis and "a touch of the cancer." Thus Callaghan assumes that he has silicosis when in fact he is diagnosed as suffering from a chronic obstructive pulmonary disease, a condition which was not compensable until 1972 (when payments were made retroactive to 1969). Although it was a change in government legislation on compensable diseases that brought Callaghan (and many other miners) under the Act, the miners assumed that the reversed decision was not the adoption of a new universalistic principle, but rather a change of mind – inexplicable and arbitrary – in each individual case.

A further matter clouding the issue is that traditionalists regard compensation as "just earnings" from their marketable commodity (their disease), whereas many medical and administrative officials regard it as but one alternative form of providing a pension. This alternative perception may explain the stance of the doctor, who suggested to Callaghan that, "if they takes the Social away from you, we'll give your Compensation.''

As a footnote to the matter of operating, I should say that some medical personnel now privately admit that the miner's rude empiricism may have been accurate in that operating may have hastened death. However, they argue that the men were almost invariably in the final stages of their disease before the operations occurred, thereby minimizing the possibility of success.

Case Four: Non-Functional Disability Classification

A. *Traditionalist perception.* Perhaps the most disturbing contradiction to the people of St. Lawrence is the non-functional classification of disability. Sammy Byrne, whose 'silicosis' is so severe that he cannot take ten steps uphill without stopping for heaving breaths, is regarded as a classic illustration of WCB underratings.

B. *Miner's perception.* "I sold me boat this morning, the first time I was without a boat since 1939. I sold it this morning. That was the hardest thing I done in me life. But I had to. I can't use her, eh? I sold me boat this morning, and all me gear. I couldn't use it, and if I couldn't use it it's no good to me. I fished twenty-six years, all me life, on top of working."

"I was rotten yesterday, and I was rotten the day before. If I does any little thing – I went down hauling in me boat and baling the water out of her – well, I never got the better of that for half the night. If I just sits down here or goes for a drive, that's fine. But if I do too much stooping or walk up the hill too fast … I've got that shifted before I realizes I shouldn't touch that. And I forgets about it, eh, cause it's not that easy to knock off working after thirty years."

"I come up (from the mine) and I was feeling miserable. I went fishing for a year and then I went back underground again. I had to walk up; I couldn't get up. I had to force meself. The last hundred feet I walked I was over an hour getting up. I had to, I had two boys going to school. I had me own home. I had to go to work. I don't care if I die in there, I'm not going to be hungry, I never growed that way. I went back before against doctor's orders, but I went back for the same reason – I knew I wasn't going to get nothing."

"I went down from roughly $7,000 last year to $75 a month compensation, and that's all I'm getting yet, and $30 from the special fund. She keeps herself see, only for the wife we would have starved to death on that. The trouble with this 30 percent, eh? We got dozens of people here 30-percent-disabled and they're going to work, same as I did. Some of these days they're going to have to bring them home same as they did me. I was feeling so miserable I wouldn't take no chance on driving the machine meself. I couldn't bring me tool box or nothing the last evening. I had to get another fellow to bring that."

"Who wants to hire you if you're 30-percent-disabled? How can you give a man a day's work with 30 percent of his lungs gone? A lot of fellows, they put on 'light duty.' So I asked the doctor, I caught him unawares I suppose,

I asked him in his opinion what would light duty be. And he told me, 'Like cleaning up fittings, painting something – I wouldn't recommend sweeping the floor, it's too dusty.' Now I spent a long time on that job and I don't see no light duty there. I don't see any place where, if I was foreman, I could give a man light duty. It's not there to give. You can't give somebody something that don't exist. Anything belonging to a mine, you needn't look for nothing under fifty pounds. Now there might be the odd job, eh? Like in the tool crib. But sure, everybody can't go in there.''

C. *Bureaucratic perception.* ''It is true that Samuel Byrne was classified as 30-percent-disabled. This was in 1972 and was based on medical evidence given the Board at that time. The diagnosis was *mild* chronic bronchitis. It was stated he was working at the time the award was made. There is nothing in Mr. Byrne's file to indicate a worsening of his condition. He has made no approach to us nor has anybody else approached us on his behalf. However, we have taken steps on our own initiative to have all workmen with chest conditions reviewed in order to re-evaluate their disabilities. It is expected that Mr. Byrne, along with all the others, will be called to St. John's shortly for examination by our medical referees.''

D. *Comment.* Community perception of Byrne's functional total disability renders insensible the WCB's classificatory system.

Case Five: The Logic of Cause and Effect

A. *Traditionalist perception.* Leonard Williams was in a mine accident in the 1940s and had to undergo many operations as a result. His breathing is so poor that he is often seen crawling out of his trap skiff and onto the pier. Yet he is classed as only 30-percent-disabled, and receives a small WCB pension which is deducted from his welfare cheque.

B. *Miner's perception.* ''I was married the 17th of July, 1940. I was working underground then and I figured I had a very good future. I didn't think the mine was going to turn out like it is, I didn't think I was going to get crippled. Life was very free with me at that time. I was in the best of health, I could haul the tail off a bull. Till I went in the mine I never had a thing wrong with me whatsoever.''

''I can't walk at all. I got to have two spells coming up here from the club; that's not very far. I can't walk aboard the skiff, I have to crawl aboard her. My legs is gone out from under me. It comes from the back, I had the back hurt in 1949 in Salt Cove Brook. Then I struck TB in the spine, but it all come from the hurt I got in the mine. I fell across the railway track and knocked me back out of place. I've went through eleven operations on that back. I'm after spending eighty-five months in hospital, in and out now.''

''I'm turned down 30 percent from the dust. But I mean I know I'm worse than 30 percent because I'm not allowed to walk from here to the shop there. From the Compensation and the Special Fund I get $152, and there's welfare on top of that. Welfare comes to $183, I think.''

"I'm after going through a world of misery now. It all come out of the mine. Ever since I got hurted in '49 I should have been paid. I got a life of misery now; as far as I'm concerned, sickness that's all my life is. I haven't got the comfort to go nowhere, I can't leave to walk nowhere, I can't go to a 'time' (party) or anything like that cause I'd have to have breath enough to do it. When I gets aboard the boat with the crowd I'm alright; well I means I goes fishing, it's the only thing I got. I got five men in the trap besides meself and they does the work and I does more or less the standing around. They knows I'm crippled up and they takes the work off me to try to help me along."

"I never had much of a life. I was only 31 years of age when I got crippled up, a young lad just in his prime. And here I am, you can say I'm almost finished. We're after having quite a time because the wife is after punching a lot of sick, I'm after punching a lot of it. We never got a break up till today."

c. *Bureaucratic perception.* Mr. Williams' accident occurred in 1949, and the W.C. Act does not compensate accidents which happened before the Act came into effect in 1951. Mr. Williams was diagnosed as minor COPD, and he was therefore given a 30-percent disability rating.

d. *Comment.* Traditionalist logic relates all Mr. Williams' complaints to the accident in the mine and cannot accept the arbitrary 1951 cut-off point. The WCB, on the other hand, is bound by bureaucratic government regulations to determine the cause-and-effect of accidents occurring after 1951.

Case Six: Pain and Discomfort
a. *Traditionalist perception.* Harry Andrews, a victim of both industrial disease and accident, has experienced continuous pain for a quarter of a century, but he received no compensation of any kind until 1972. This is seen as a classic case of WCB indifference to the community's suffering.

b. *Miner's perception.* "I had the accident in '44. The roof come down on me, a big slab. Joe Malone makes a screech at me to get out of the way. If I'd stayed where I was at, probably I wouldn't have got hurted – or perhaps I would have got killed. When he made a screech, I made a jump, and I jumped right under her. I could feel the shattering down over me, that's all I knows. I felt it first hitting the hat to smithereens. And that's all I knows. I went out cold then and didn't know nothing else."

"After I got to St. John's, the nurses there didn't think I was going to get better. The doctor thought it too. The shovel went into me side, they said, and I was busted open and me hip was all crushed up. Me leg was broke. I was all beat up down around me privates. The pelvis, that got bent in and never come out. I'm different on one side than on the other see."

"I couldn't make no water. They had to put a tube into me stomach. I still couldn't do it when I come home, I still can't do it. I got to lie down. Whenever I wants to make me water, I got to lie down. They never cured me if I'm still like that, did they? I goes through more pain, me son, with that. I figures there's only one more fellow ever suffered more than I'm after suffering, and that's Jesus Christ. And that was only while He was carrying the cross and dying on it. But I'm at it this last thirty years. When I wants to make me water, I go in there and stand over that toilet. I could be there an hour before a drop came. When it do come, perhaps it'd be drop drop drop. And I have the worst kind of pain while that's going on. Same as you had a cramp in your stomach. Well that's the way I be all the time.''

"The way it is with me water, I can't make me water and I can't hold it. I'm right bursting to do that now. Say I were ready to do it and somebody in the bathroom. I'd be right busting to do it and wouldn't be able to hold it dropping out of me. I used to spoil more shorts like that; they'd get soaking wet and I'd take them off and heave them away and go get another pair. I'd be right busting to do it and it'd be right dropping out of me, dropping out of me. I'd get in and stand up over the tub. I'd be going mad with the pain, and still the same, just dropping. The doctor told me they made a false passage up through me. He said, 'That'll gradually close up on you.' ''

c. *Bureaucratic perception.* The Newfoundland WCB does not compensate for pain and discomfort. This position is expressed in terms of the difficulty of distinguishing real pain from malingering; two men can have the same trauma, yet one will say he is suffering terribly while the other not even mention his discomfort. This attitude is given scientific sanction by the WCB's use of one of the standard U.S. medical reference works (Kessler, 1970:157–58) which refers to the problem in the following terms : "One of the most difficult symptoms to evaluate is that of pain. The patient may claim inability to work because of 'pain' on any part of the body. One may regard the claim as a self-serving declaration like the indicted criminal who 'claims' that he is innocent. Many patients have a psychological need for the pain and hence do not want it to disappear ... the patient with chronic suffering may claim to desire relief while really hoping to hold onto the pain.''

d. *Comment.* The divergence between traditionalist medicine and bureaucratic folk-psychiatry clearly reflects conflicting vested interests; yet neither has any special claim to legitimacy. Regardless, such a situation exacerbates the hostility and incomprehension between traditionalists and bureaucrats.

Communication Between Cosmologies

It is not only the ideational systems which are mutually incomprehensible. Less important perhaps, but significantly divisive, are the incompatible languages used by traditionalists and bureaucrats to communicate. (A discussion of this issue is reserved for the following chapter on the face-to-face encounter between bureaucrat and traditionalist.) But given the 450-

mile return journey between St. Lawrence and St. John's, much of the communication necessarily takes place by mail. The essence of this postal dissonance is that the traditionalists, who are often illiterate and must dictate their letters to school children, attempt to argue their case in personalistic terms as befits their cosmology. Yet the replies they receive from the WCB, shaped as they are by government regulations and the bureaucratic cosmology, are written in a language whose depersonalization is interpreted as a direct insult. Compare, for example, the following letters from a single file. The first is a letter – the beginnings of an attempt to obtain compensation – written by a disabled miner to his patron, the M.H.A., who in turn passed the letter on to the WCB. (My own emphasis is put on the personalistic statements.)

I wish to bring to your attention that the Relieving Officer was to visit me Saturday and he told me I would have to report to work to Burin for working on fish plant. I told him I was drawing unemployment and he asked me if it was enough to live on, and *I said no*. He said he wouldn't be able to make up my order. He also told me if I went to Burin and only made $50 if my order is $200 he would make up the rest. At present *I am sick*, *I worked 12 years underground* so I decided to go to the doctor before I reported for work in Burin. So the doctor sent me home for two weeks rest, and then go back to him again. He told me *my chest was in very bad state* and inclined to think *I could have what the miners got*. *I'm almost fifty years old I have to leave my home with a family of ten for two or three days a week* in a plant at Burin – *after working hard all my life time looking after my family, I don't think this is very considerate. I was a 'Liberal' all my life*. If I had a good job steady work suitable to *my health and age* I really can't go to sea nor work in a fish plant now. *My nerves are poor*. Kindly reply to me immediately as I need a reply to show to relieving officer on the 1st of Feb by letter or wire. *What is the difference in making up the Assistance with Unemployment as making up with part time work*? Thanks for immediate reply.

The miner, who was not to be compensated for another four years, makes thirteen personalistic points in a 300-word letter. He begins with his precarious financial position and goes on to discuss his physical and mental condition; he stresses his personal worth and his political loyalty to his patron's party. He argues that two reasons exist for the reversal of his present position: the first is that his present treatment by government agencies is not "very considerate," and the second is that no real distinctions exist between public funding ("unemployment") and "part-time work" in the publicly subsidized fish plants. The latter argument is inherent in the traditionalist's conception of public agencies as exploitable resources, just as fishing, logging, and farming are to those who make their living exploiting nature.[8]

The following letter is the WCB's response, rejecting the miner's claim for compensation after his examination in St. John's.

Dear Sir,
   Your claim for Workmen's Compensation benefits has been placed before the Silicosis Referee Board which was appointed under authority of the Workmen's Compensation Act.

Having considered and evaluated all the evidence the Board's conclusion is that you do not suffer from any industrial disease. There is no evidence at all to support a diagnosis of either silicosis or cancer of the lung.

In a very important way this will undoubtedly be welcome news to you. On the other hand, since you may be subject to a general condition which cannot be classed as an industrial disease we regret that, in view of the findings, you have no entitlement to Workmen's Compensation benefits. The findings of the Referee Board must be accepted by this Board.

This letter, written in words which most miners have never seen or heard before, makes several points when interpreted across the barrier of the traditionalist cosmology. In the eyes of the miner, that he does "not suffer from any industrial disease" is an outright lie. Whereas the WCB was quite justified in making this statement in terms of the medical and bureaucratic criteria accepted at the time, the miner makes no distinction between chronic obstructive pulmonary disease (which he had) and silicosis. Indeed, miners call them by the same name; their symptoms are the same, and to them, it is "the miner's disease." The second point, that "in a very important way this will undoubtedly be welcome news to you" is singularly divisive: the bureaucrats are bewildered when miners are "disappointed" that they have no industrial disease, and often assume that the miners must be "so obsessed" with money that "nothing else matters." Yet in traditionalist ethnomedicine, all illnesses suffered by miners are the "miner's disease" and all lead to an early death.[9] Thus this statement is seen as an intolerable insult and the conclusion as despicable hypocrisy, for the miner's economic life is now over, and the WCB has refused him a dignified "wage" for his disease.

The third letter, reprinted below, illustrates the tone and style of discourse used with pensioners in response to their queries.

Dear Sir,[10]

This is in reply to your letter of July 21, 1975 regarding your pension payments.

As of November 20, 1972, you received a pension from this Board of $187.50 per month. This was increased July 1, 1973 to $250.00 per month.

An amendment to the Workmen's Compensation Act, also during July 1973, provided that in the case of permanent total disability (100% disability) the Board could pay a monthly pension to a workman not less than that payable to a widow with the same number of dependent children.

At that time, a widow was receiving $150 per month, plus $50.00 for each dependent child. The child's allowance ceasing at age 16, but continuing to age 21, if he continued to further his education.

So that you could receive maximum benefits under our Act, your pension was temporarily reduced to $150.00 per month. For each of your eight children you received $50.00. Instead of $250.00 per month, the Board was then able to pay you $550.00 per month.

The Board is pleased to advise that as a result of a recent amendment to the Act, your pension is to be increased from $150.00 per month to $225.00 per month. For each of your 7 dependent children, you will still receive $50.00. Your pension payments as of August 1975, will thus be in the amount of $575.00.

In accordance with the Workmen's Compensation Act, as each child finishes his education,

your payments will be reduced by $50.00. Please be assured, however, that your monthly payments will not be reduced below $300.00.
  We trust this will clarify the situation for you ...

In each case then, communication between the cosmologies is couched in a language quite inappropriate to the receiver, languages which are inevitably misinterpreted across the ideological barrier. As such, the language of communication is an additional element in the construction of mutual incomprehensibility.

Critical Contradictions
WCB officials are in an impossible 'double bind' in which they are required to execute regulations that are essentially contradictory and unintegrated, on behalf of people who are incapable of accepting the WCB's particular universalistic and impersonalistic regulations.

Although its intention may be to compensate all justifiable cases, the Workmen's Compensation Act and its many amendments have not been treated by the legislators as an integrated organic whole. Consequently, little attention has been paid to the relationships between the different amendments and to the differential impact of the stipulations of the Act on the population. Each major amendment has brought new categories of disabled workers and widows under compensation; but in doing so, it has 'discriminated' against other categories. The original 1951 Act compensated silicosis victims only; but true silicosis is rare in St. Lawrence, and hence, the Act left uncompensated and embittered all those with other mine diseases, as well as the wives of men who died before the Act went into effect in 1951. The 1960 amendment, which added lung cancer caused by underground radiation to the list, still excluded pre-'51 workers, surface workers, and sufferers from heart conditions and COPD. Twelve years (and a new government) ensued before COPD was brought under the Act – thirteen years before surface and pre-'51 workers were compensated, and before pension rates were unilaterally increased. And it was not until 1975 that a wide range of cancers became compensable. Even at this writing, however, only heart disease associated with silicosis is compensable.

Despite the amendments, important discriminations still remain in the form of bureaucratic regulations which are incompatible with traditionalist logical modes. Perhaps the greatest source of incongruity is the system of partial disability ratings which are based entirely on non-economic criteria: for approximately half of those rated as partially disabled and who are unable to perform alternative work, the compensation cheque *has no value whatsoever*, for they are forced to live on welfare, and the Department of Social Assistance simply deducts the value of the WCB cheque from its own. The formula for calculating the partial disability pension (for a 30-percent disability, the formula is 30 percent of 75 percent of the maximum

wage permitted by the WCB in the year the miner was "turned down")
keeps the 'income' small, yet infinitely diverse. The absence of inflation
indexing makes the process more intense.

The lack of congruity with communal ethnomedicine creates confusion
about heart disease which is associated by the people with COPD (called
silicosis by the miners), but which is not compensable, and heart disease
associated with "true silicosis," which is compensable. The refusal to
recognize pain and discomfort (accepted by some provincial boards and not
others) as a compensable condition leads to anomalies: men who manage to
force themselves to work until retirement receive no recompense; the
ineligibility of pre-'51 accident cases renders some totally disabled men (for
example, those who are 70-percent-disabled from pre-'51 accidents, 30-
percent-disabled from COPD) permanently restricted to small partial disability pensions. Finally, some men are potentially worth more dead than
alive: if a miner on partial disability, living on a combination of compensation and welfare, dies of cancer, his widow is entitled to receive the full
WCB pension. If she has many children living with her, it can double her
previous income.

These anomalies and discriminations, based on what are, in St. Lawrence, essentially 'foreign' distinctions, together with the catalogue of
twenty-five years of perceived irrationality and injustice, exacerbate the
lack of communication and keep filled-to-brimming the well of bitterness in
St. Lawrence and Lawn.

THE ENCOUNTER: THE DANCE OF IRRELEVANCE

The order of events leading up to a confrontation with the WCB involves an
about-face in the miner's presentation of self. When a miner first begins to
realize that he is developing the well-known symptoms of "the mine
disease," that he is getting "a touch of the dust," his initial tactics are to
conceal this fact from the world. He does not tell his family, for no man will
burden his family with this knowledge until it is inescapable. He conceals
his symptoms as best he can from the doctors and from his employers
because to reveal his growing disability to them is to write *finis* to his
normal economic life. His economic game plan is dictated by the fact that
once he is officially classified as disabled and "turned down" from work
underground, the chances of his finding alternative long-term employment
are poor. He therefore loses not only his wages, high by St. Lawrence
standards, but also his position as a respectable and hard-working individual; most disabled miners must take welfare payments as well as compensation, thereby lowering their social status to "welfare family." Thus
he drives himself to conceal the symptoms of his disease, to stifle his
coughs and his anxiety, and to maintain a minimum work load in the face of

increasing breathlessness, dizziness, and his sense of impending doom. If he is lucky and determined, if the progress of his disease is revealed but slowly on the annual X-Rays, he might be able to maintain this façade for several years. This delay is critical, as being "turned down" signals a triple degradation of his persona – his body, economic position, and social status.

Inevitably, however, the time comes when the afflicted miner can maintain this position no longer. His will and physique collapse, or his medical examinations betray his secret, and he is "turned down" from underground work. Because the possibilities for alternative employment are extremely limited,[11] he must now prepare for the battle with the WCB. His labour is no longer a marketable commodity: the sole source of his economic and social dignity is now his disease. His economic game plan is now dedicated to obtaining a 100-percent total disability rating from the WCB – with that rating's generous pension benefits. If he obtains *anything* less than a 100-percent rating, the pension has no value since he is "turned over to Welfare" for part of his income, and to add insult to injury, suffer the stigma implicit in becoming a "welfare family." His tactics must now be reversed – from denying his sickness altogether to maximizing the world's perception of his disease and its symptoms.

The goal is clear and the penalty for failure is high. Now begins the process of interviews with the local doctors, referrals to St. John's hospitals, the 450-mile return journeys to St. John's, and consultations with the WCB. The miner's sense of the justice of his cause is buttressed by the knowledge that in traditionalist terms, he is functionally totally disabled – he is no longer able to work because of "the mine disease." But a sense of futility may pervade his spirit since he knows that he has less than one chance in three of obtaining a total-disability rating.[12]

Under these circumstances he begins his battle with the WCB, fighting with a bureaucracy which, from his distillation of traditionalist lore, he "knows" is dedicated to denying him his "proper entitlement." He does not understand which matters are fixed by law (for example, lung cancer) and which are in fact negotiable (especially partial disability pensions). Nor does he understand the rules of the battle: still a creature of a world view which conceives of power relations in personalistic terms, he must confront in their munificent offices the doctors and bureaucrats who speak in words he has never heard, and make decisions on the basis of criteria he cannot accept. The skills he requires for this he does not have: dressing in order to impress, controlling his emotions, being dishonest in ways which demonstrate ambition and initiative. These are part of the bureaucratic world with which he has had little contact. He believes his ammunition to be the array of patrons he can marshall and his intimate knowledge of the operations of the WCB. But the former – the local doctor, the lawyer, the priest, and the M.H.A. – must operate in terms of their own constructs and limitations; and the latter is primarily a storehouse of misinformation seen through the distorting prism of traditionalist conceptions. With such dubious ammunition he, nonetheless, sets out to do battle with "the Compensation."

The encounter itself, between miner and WCB official, is governed by rules which participants only imperfectly understand, for mutual deception and manipulation are the tactics each side must employ, and the two parties negotiate in incompatible coinage. Indeed, there is a surrealistic quality to these encounters, for the two actors are playing out quite different social dramas. The disabled worked is playing client in a patron-client scenario, which he interprets as his opportunity to alter the WCB's decision. The official, for his part, is playing administrator in a bureaucratic scenario, which he sees as his opportunity to justify the WCB's decision.

To this end, WCB officials use a series of bureaucratic blocks and counter-strikes to control the assaults of the traditionalists during these encounters. Their primary tactics are 1) *emotive distraction*: trotting out, literally or verbally, blinded youths and armless men to convince the claimant that he is "feeling sorry for himself"; 2) *bureaucratizing*: reeling off rules and regulations, using bureaucratic jargon, and displaying incomprehensible charts with percentage ratings and anatomical drawings; 3) *boardizing*: the various uses of "Board" either to give greater weight to a decision, or to displace responsibility; 4) *distancing*: removing self from the consequences of the decision, as when doctors say they only make the percentage ratings and have "nothing to do with the money – that's the Board's responsibility," while the claims officers have "nothing to do with the percentage ratings" – that's fixed by the Doctors – and only calculate the pensions; 5) *aggression blocking*: the use of the open office and the female employees to minimize the claimant's displays of aggression.

The scales, then, are heavily weighted in favour of the officials, for the battle is played according to their rules. The traditionalists' personalistic attacks are invariably blocked by the bureaucrat, since only the WCB official has the experience and the time to develop a repertoire of such counter-moves.[13] In this sense then, the encounter is a dance of irrelevance.

A Traditionalist Assault: Failure
The scene is the Claims Room: a large office occupied by a WCB Claims officer and his cohort of perhaps a dozen female employees. The officer, his desk and chairs are screened in one corner by glass floor-to-eye-level walls. Outside the Claims Room, beside the reception desk, sits a claimant, Pete Hodder. Hodder has just been notified that despite his best efforts, he has been classified as 30-percent-disabled because of COPD, and that his

permanent pension will accordingly be less than $180 per month. Although the decision is presented to him as final, he in fact has several options, the most obvious and immediate of which is to protest the decision. Hodder moves up to the reception desk, demanding in a loud and angry voice to "see the Claims Officer." The secretary, obviously unnerved by the tone of his request – inappropriate in all circumstances to the bureaucratic style, but appropriate in some traditionalist contexts – steps through a door leading to the Claims Room, and warns a senior officer that "you'd better see this man – he's saucy." The interview takes place in eighteen basic moves: in strikes, blocks, and counter-strikes.

1. TRADITIONALIST THREAT. Hodder, a large and powerful man, enters the Claims Officer's (C.O.) partitioned nook in a rage. The C.O.'s face reveals anxiety about the possibility that Hodder "might get violent."

2. TRADITIONALIST ASSAULT. "Here, you can have this goddam cheque back!" Slams cheque on C.O.'s desk. "It's no fucking good to me. You except me to live on this? Jesus!"

3. BUREAUCRAT'S BLOCK. Moved to reduce the tension, the C.O. speaks in a cajoling, non-aggressive tone: a counter-threat is impossible, as it would guarantee physical violence. He therefore appeals to an outside source, compromising the position of neither Hodder nor himself. "Easy now, there's girls in this office, they can all hear you. There can't be any swearing with them hearing you." Hodder is blocked, and cannot pursue his assault without compromising his decency *vis-à-vis* the women.

4. BUREAUCRAT'S CONSOLIDATION. The C.O. consolidates control by suggesting that if Hodder behaves according to WCB rules, he might be helped: "I'll be glad to discuss your case with you, but it's got to be calm." Thus the worker's assault is utterly neutralized by an appeal to chivalry and then suggestion, or hint, of the possibility of repairing matters.

5. TRADITIONALIST'S FIRST ARGUMENT: a personalistic argument: "You can't expect me to live on $180 a month. There's no way I can live on $180!"

6. BUREAUCRAT'S RESPONSE. The C.O. continues the conciliation through apparent identification. "No, of course you can't. I couldn't live on it, and there's no way you could live on it."

7. TRADITIONALIST ELABORATES ARGUMENT. Hodder spins out his initial argument, elaborating on the personalistic. "I've got a wife and three youngsters and a house to pay for – I can't do that on 180 bucks." Hodder's tone is decreasingly hostile.

8. BUREAUCRAT'S RESPONSE. Having established a minimum level of identification, the C.O. shifts to bureaucratic criteria in order to gambit

the worker and block his whole line of argument. "Absolutely not, no way. I see that. But the Board isn't set up to support you. That's the law."

9. TRADITIONALIST'S SECOND ARGUMENT: Attempt to extract the bureaucrat's sympathy for his personal tragedy. "What do you think it's like with this silicosis, wheezing away. How'd you like it?"

10. BUREAUCRAT'S RESPONSE. This standard argument is blocked in a standard fashion (emotive distraction): attention is drawn to another, much more tragic case than the claimant's, who "happens to be in the office right now," or was there "only a short while ago." For example, "There's a young boy out in that office right now, 19 years old, had to be led in by his wife: he was blinded when his jackhammer hit a stick of dynamite. There's lots worse off than you." The traditionalist can only agree that there are "lots worse off than me," and his ploy is blunted.

11. TRADITIONALIST'S THIRD ARGUMENT. Hodder is now blocked from direct hostility and from personalistic criteria, and resorts to displaced threat to indicate the seriousness of his stance. "I'm an ex-con you know, and I'll go back there before I try to live on *that*."

12. BUREAUCRAT'S RESPONSE. Freed from his concern over violence and not required to respond to Hodder's third argument, the C.O. can now consolidate a stance of helpfulness and objectivity and use this position to expand his argument. "Here, let me see your file." The C.O. shuffles papers and leafs through the file, asking the worker to summarize his case and promising to do whatever he can.

13. TRADITIONALIST'S PROPOSITION. Knowing that inflation will quickly reduce the value of the monthly $180 and that if he cannot find work, the Department of Welfare will deduct the $180 from his welfare cheque, Hodder takes the sensible option and asks that his pension reserve be turned over to him in a lump sum. "That 180 bucks is no good to me. I want a lump sum."

14. BUREAUCRAT'S COUNTER. The C.O. first introduces impersonal bureaucratic criteria and then displaces responsibility onto the Board (bureaucratizing and boardizing), in both cases divorcing himself from the decision. "Well, you're classified as 30-percent-disabled, and the Board doesn't give lump sum payments for anybody over 10 percent." He overcommunicates the rigidity of the Board and the Law, hoping to stop matters here. "Look, we don't get our jollies by withholding your money, you know. But we've got government rules and regulations on how we're allowed to disburse our money."

15. TRADITIONALIST'S RESPONSE. Moving on to the defensive, Hodder acts to apologize without apologizing. "I see that. Don't get me wrong now. I'm not mad at you, it's the Board. All I want is what's due me, that's all." Thus he emphasizes his essential reasonableness.

16. BUREAUCRAT'S ASSAULT. Sensing Hodder's increasing defensiveness, the C.O. moves to close his argument. He does so first by
referring to government regulations, and then by standard obfuscation.
"It's bad, but it's all you're entitled to, under the Act. That's the Law.
$180." Pointing to a drawing of a hand, with each portion of the hand
labelled according to percentage disability and covered with Latin
names for each bone and joint, he says: "Here, look at this. See, if you
lose the tip of a finger, that's a certain percentage, and if you lose your
metacarpal, that's another percentage. That's the Law. The Law says
you're 30-percent-disabled, and so you're entitled to 30 percent of 75
percent of the maximum permitted wages at the time you were laid
off."
17. TRADITIONALIST CAPITULATES. "I see that." His face, manner, and
voice are depressed, defeated.
18. BUREAUCRAT CONSOLIDATES VICTORY. In the same sentence, the
C.O. commiserates with Hodder and brings the encounter to a conclusion. "I'd like to do more for you: I know you can't live on that. But
that's all the Law allows. I'll keep workings on it for you."

   Comment. The Claims Officer's purpose *vis-à-vis* the Board, in this
particular case, is first to neutralize any potential aggression – always a fear
among WCB employees – and second, to protect the Board from having to
deal with the case. He legitimizes their original decision by planting firmly
in Hodder's mind the notions that the Board reached its decision entirely
according to the law, and by suggesting that there can be no further appeal
(this is inaccurate) at present but that he might be able to negotiate something better in the future (this is unlikely).

   The traditionalist's misperception of the encounter caused him first to
use inappropriate and ineffective weapons – threats and personalistic appeals – and then to miss the fact that the decision was made by Claims and
Medical personnel and not by the Board. (Therefore, Hodder was in fact
free to appeal the decision to the Board.) This latter point is frequently
missed, as workers do not distinguish between the different levels of WCB
employees, and WCB personnel consciously further this confusion. The
bureaucrat's weapons – the girls, the law, sympathy, and obfuscation –
allow him to block the threat, counter the arguments, and close the case.

Victory Through Legislative Change
The majority of widows and disabled miners who "won their battle" with
the WCB and are now receiving 100-percent disability pensions did not
achieve this on the basis of their efforts to do so. Rather, the successive
amendments to the 1951 Act kept Newfoundland in line with other Canadian provinces, and brought new classes of diseases and workers under the
terms of the Act. But the traditionalists are frequently unaware of this and

regard their sudden inclusion not as the carrying out of new universalistic principles, but as the just conclusion to their individual battles with the Board. Indeed, the majority of disabled miners presently receiving pensions were compensated only in 1972, when an amendment to the Act accepted chronic obstructive pulmonary disease as industry-linked, and therefore compensable. The newly compensated miner and his family see this victory as the WCB's relenting in their personal battle with him. Among the devices the miner turned to – and which he feels brought him victory – were prayer and membership in a religious society. Direct pressuring of medical and political patrons to act on his behalf and unrelenting pressure on the WCB have already been mentioned. "It took me five years. I found them all in St. John's: Confederation Building, the Philip Building, statues and everything else. I used to come and check them every day. I never give them no breaks at all. I just kept right on their backs and somebody had to do something pretty soon. I knew that was me money."

Roche Manning, a 48-year-old miner, was no longer able to work by 1968. In his perception of events, it took him four years of battle with the WCB, hectoring his patrons, praying for divine intercession ("the wife belongs to the St. Anne's Society: St. Anne's is very good, she's been good to us before"), before the WCB acquiesced. This occurred, Manning believes, when the WCB finally gave up demanding proof (in the form of an operation) that he had silicosis, and "realized" that he had it.

In fact, Manning never had silicosis; rather, in 1968, WCB doctors diagnosed chronic obstructive pulmonary disease. A letter to Manning from the WCB at that time rejected his claim for compensation on the grounds that he had neither lung cancer nor silicosis, the only diseases compensable at that time. During the next four years, Manning says he continued his efforts on all fronts. The 1969 Royal Commission completed its investigation of the St. Lawrence tragedy, and among its many recommendations was that COPD be made a compensable disease. After the Liberal regime was removed from office in 1972, the appropriate action was taken. COPD was made a compensable industrial disease, and the many miners suffering from the ailment were recalled to the WCB for fresh examination. An official notification of this new decision went to Manning: "The Board, after a careful study of all the medical evidence presented, have rated you to be 100 percent disabled. Cheques in the amount of $86.54[14] will be mailed to you every two weeks commencing 4 Sept. 1972." Although the WCB letter said clearly that the fresh evaluation was a consequence of the amendment to the Act, Manning had no doubt that the letter was an apology from the WCB for their previous "mistake," and his victory a direct consequence of his traditionalist manipulations.[15]

Victory Through "Benefit of the Doubt"
On the 10th of May, 62-year-old Bob O'Neill slipped and fell, hurting his

back; a month later, he submitted a claim to the WCB. The WCB noted, "You did not report your accident to your employer or seek medical attention until May 21," and asked for an explanation of the delay. "At this point," said the Claims Officer in retrospect, "there are two ways of looking at this: why shouldn't we just give the worker the benefit of the doubt, or why don't we stop potential abuse and make the worker realize there's no room for fiddling – everything must be done right." In the O'Neill case, the initial decision was for the latter course of action.

On July 19, Bob O'Neill sent the WCB his explanation. The officer commented: "Our doctors liked this letter. We wondered who wrote it." The letter from O'Neill, clearly written by a patron, ran ... "We were in the act of hoisting a large valve when I slipped. I did not realize that I was seriously hurt, although my mates saw what happened. I thought what pain I had would pass off in a day or two. But it didn't and on the 21st I decided I would have to seek medical attention for whatever injury I had done. Sure I realize now that I should have gone to the Doctor immediately. But I was not convinced that it was serious enough for me to have to quit work, so I tried to carry on in the interest of my job." From the officer's perspective, the letter is excellent in that it gives a "legitimate" reason for the delay, and shows that the worker is "not a slacker." Both the officer and the WCB medical staff recommended that they "render benefit of the doubt in claimant's favour. However, such a claim should be kept under extremely close review, especially in view of the claimant's age." O'Neill was placed on a temporary total disability pension, pending his return to health.

However, in August, when O'Neill was showing no sign of recovery, X-Rays showed "degenerative osteoarthritis of the spine," suggesting the possibility that his "condition did not result from trauma (the fall) at all" and that he may not really be eligible for compensation. The officer grew suspicious of O'Neill's claim at this point, but said "it becomes a medical question, and it's not for a Claims Officer to make a decision." More consultants were brought in to review the case and to reach some conclusion.

O'Neill was hospitalized on the 21st of September and discharged one week later. A medical report noted that a barium enema revealed a hernia: "this of course is a very long standing condition and need not be related in any way to this man's pain or his fall back in May." O'Neill's payments were then withheld. On November 11th, he wrote the WCB: "I have not received any benefit from you since Sept. 20th. I fully intend coming in to see you the latter part of this week, and I shall expect a more human touch than you have given me. I am not one to sham sick, it is just not like me to do it. I have a hard family to support, and I do want to work." O'Neill's appointment with the Claims Officer is arranged for November 17th.

Waiting for the interview, the C.O. confesses to a feeling of unease regarding O'Neill's potential aggressiveness in this interview. However, he is favourably disposed to the case on the basis of O'Neill's consistent expression of one of the WCB's prime morals – the work ethic. "The guy's a pretty good sort – good character – you have a little more sympathy perhaps." He notes that O'Neill could have applied for welfare, but didn't and dipped into his own savings while waiting for compensation.

Claims officers frequently complain that claimants have difficulty in conveying any information, let alone the information the bureaucrats wish to hear. Indeed, "sometimes the only way you can get anything out of them is by going down their throats and hauling it out yourself." In this case, because the C.O. is favourably disposed towards O'Neill, he wants O'Neill to provide information he can use on his behalf. In the interview, however, O'Neill does not oblige. Dressed in an unpressed and out-of-fashion brown suit, running shoes, and a nylon hunting cap which he nervously twists, O'Neill insists upon arguing in traditionalist terms, continually referring to his state of "nerves"; "I'm depressed, very depressed. The doctor says so, and he's given me a lot of pills to take for my depression." As he says this, his face takes on an exaggeratedly depressed appearance. At the same time, he resorts to the other traditionalist ploys of displacing aggression (vituperatively blaming the doctors for the delays), and referring to the difficulties of raising his family.

In passing, he mentions the steel floor on which he fell. The C.O. zeros in on the "steel," asking: "Why didn't you mention it was steel in your report?" Steel is a significant additive in that it *sounds* as if it is more damaging to tissue and bone, thereby enabling the C.O. to offer this as new evidence. The C.O. pursued his 'advantage': did Mr. O'Neill feel that his hernia was related to work? O'Neill said yes. The C.O. then left the interview to make a final consultation with the WCB doctor.

"I had this pretty well sized-up before I went in to the doctor; he more or less went along with it." Indeed, the course of decision-making is such that when the officer or doctor makes a decision, the other frequently "goes along with it" despite the status differential between them. Thus although a C.O. must always defer to a doctor, if the C.O. is committed to a decision, the doctor will normally concur. "Even though he's got an underlying condition, if an accident aggravates a condition, we accept the claim." In O'Neill's case, the doctor agreed, and felt that "we're stuck with this, we've got to pay this man. We've got to pay this man for the hernia by rendering him all benefit of doubt."

O'Neill was called in and told that his final claim was accepted, but that the WCB would not be responsible for any further recurring condition: "We don't like to leave them with the idea that every time they get a bit of back pain, we're responsible. You'd be surprised how many workmen get back pain, and even years later, they figure we're responsible." "This could blow up a little bit more though. Remember he said he wasn't feeling good, and they're having a lay-off now … I've been suckered in before."

Comment. Government and WCB regulations state that in dubious cases, the benefit of the doubt must be rendered to the workmen. But the manner in which legitimate doubt is established is often not a function of any objective criteria: in the O'Neill case, further medical opinions on any possible link between the fall and the hernia should have been required. It was decided not to pursue additional medical opinions, partially because they would be opinions only, but primarily because the claimant had revealed himself as a "man of good character," one who embraced the WCB's work ethic. O'Neill's victory, then, was a consequence of this ploy, contained in 'his' letter (clearly written by a patron, who understood or stumbled upon the values according to which the WCB operates). His own comments were ignored.

Victory Through Metamorphosis: Profession of the Bureaucratic World View

ACT ONE

The Scene: the luxurious private office of a member of the Board. To his front and his right are two padded armchairs; to his left a simple chrome chair to which the claimant will be directed. The claimant, Vincent Malraux, suffered a back injury the previous year, and has been on a temporary total disability pension since then. Recently learning that his pension, which was enough for him to live on, is to be stopped because his back had healed, and that he is to be turned over to a permanent partial disability pension of 15 percent ($80 per month for life), he has decided to protest the WCB's decision. He has chosen to appeal the decision and request instead that his pension be commuted and he be given a lump-sum payment. Malraux's personal background makes him marginal to the traditionalist world. Himself a foreman and the son of an entrepreneur, he completed grade seven and spent several years working in Toronto. For him, the transition from traditionalist to bureaucrat is already advanced. Malraux is waiting outside at the reception desk, and seated in the office are Commissioner I and the ethnographer. Commissioner I is reviewing Malraux's file, looking for pertinent cues.

Comm I: "Hmm. Rehabilitation saw Malraux a while ago and asked him to upgrade himself [that is, obtain vocational training] but Malraux showed no interest at all. All he said to rehab was, "What happens then?" [even with new training, he would probably still be unemployed]. [Cue 1. His attitude is therefore negative.] "Malraux wants a lump sum. The actuarial tables would give him a pension of $35,000 over his lifetime, but he'd only get about half of that in a lump sum. He'd probably blow it all this winter living like a king, and then he'll be broke. And maybe his back will get worse in six months, and he'll want back on compensation then, but he'll have lost his pension." [Cue 2. His proposition is probably based on unrealistic attitudes, and is therefore negative.] "Did you see him in the hall? That's a $140 overcoat. He's been working while getting temporary total." Thumbs through file. "We have information he's been working." [Cue 3. His behaviour, although not illegal, seems dishonest.] [Cue 4. Commissioner notes that Malraux has been off work for a year.] Therefore according to U.S. statistics, "there is a 90% chance he'll never work again. [Cue 5. is also negative.] The company didn't hire him back, so he's probably not a very good worker." Cue 6. "And he's very negative about upgrading or improving himself." "But we'll see if his ideas are sound. Maybe we'll cover a loan for him at the bank. We'll see what he's like: sometimes you get a good impression."

Comment: The Commissioner is trying to assess the case. In doing so, he observes items of behaviour which conflict with WCB values, such as Malraux's unwillingness to "improve himself." He also places a negative evaluation on behaviours which are theoretically neutral or, as we shall see, which are capable of being transformed from negative to positive – as in his alleged employment while receiving a temporary total pension.

Enter Malraux, displaying slight nervousness but speaking in reasonable and confident tones. Commissioner I and Malraux shake hands and are seated. Commissioner I reinforces the moral/social superiority of his status by an introductory chat pierced with strongly worded questions with hints of accusation delivered in a disinterested tone, coupled with sudden withdrawals of all interest and conversation.

Comm I: *How's the back?* In a bored, disbelieving tone.

Malraux: *It's not as good as it was before. Last week I felt it while I was walking. I got very concerned and made an appointment with the doctor.* Malraux is already feinting well; he is communicating that his injury is not only severe, but that his back is getting worse, and that if his needs are not met now, he might press for more. An excellent opening move.

Comm I: Thinking, he later confessed to the ethnographer, "they all try that one." *What's the cause of it?*

Malraux: *Something I might have done? It was like it was catching in the back.* He continues hinting that his injury may be intensifying. Commissioner I, in retrospect, laughed and said, "What's he going to say, 'it's getting better,' so we can cut off his pension?"

Comm I: With an ambiguous hint of commiseration and suspicion. *It's a pretty tricky thing, the back.* Trying to put Malraux on the defensive, he asks, *Can't work at all?*

Malraux: *I've tried it, but a bit of lifting, or tying my shoes, and it'll [the pain] come.*

Comm I: Trying to play down severity. *No steady pain?*

Malraux: *An ache.*

Comm I: *You're comfortable lying down, though.*

Malraux: *No.*

Comm I: Blocked. *No? We'll wait for the other commissioner.* Long silence. Enter Commissioner II. Shakes hands with Malraux, and sits down. To emphasize his status and his disinterest in the drama, he notices a man passing in the hall (the door has been left ajar) and begins a two-minute conversation with him about "the meter" which is incomprehensible to everyone in the room. Commissioner I and Malraux stare off blankly. Commissioner II returns his attention to the room.

Comm I: Speaking in judge-like tones, he moves to minimize injury and to foreclose the WCB's obligations. *Mr. Malraux, as far as the Board is concerned, you've reached maximum benefits and you're 15-percent disabled. In other words, you're 85-percent able.* His reversal of figures is meant to minimize the injury. *It's our responsibility to pay you a 15-percent permanent partial disability pension, and that's what we intend to do.* Emphasizing pointlessness of Malraux's bothering to change their mind. *We can't pay you temporary total disability anymore. This'll* (permanent partial) *be payable to you for the rest of your life* (stressing WCB generosity and good sense). *I understand you want to appeal this decision: on what grounds? And is there anything else you want us to do?*

Malraux: Strikes again, and throws Commissioners off their stride by suggesting a WCB irregularity. *About this 15-percent disability: I was never informed of that.* Commissioners exchange looks. Hurried consultation between them, shuffling through files. They finally conclude, uneasily, that Malraux's lateness of notification is unfortunate (Commissioner II blames the postal strike, but Commissioner I says they could have phoned: the two end up blaming the Claims Officers). But nothing can be done, and he knows about the decision now.

Comm I: Invoking medical sanction, *Our doctors at the Board have reviewed this case and our doctors say your back can't get any worse and it can't get any better. So what can we do?*

Comm II: Invoking government sanction, *we have scheduled the ratings; it's the same all across Canada. You're the same as the fellow with a few fingers gone.* Commissioner II is emphasizing the scientific soundness of their procedures.

Malraux: First attempt at a personal assault. *You don't know what it feels like.*

Comm II: Easily deflecting accusation by reference to science and law: *We don't go on what you feel. We go on our schedule. The doctors make up the schedule.*

Malraux: Weakly, *a doctor couldn't tell me what I feel.*

Comm I: Switching conversation as present theme unfruitful. *What can you do?*

Malraux: Returns to point which weakened Commissioners. *I just found out last week* [about the termination of the temporary total pension]. *They left me in a pretty awkward position. I've got eight youngsters and Christmas is coming up.* The latter comment is personalistic and useless, but does not negate the former. There is a further exchange of forms and files between the Commissioners, obviously put off by this problem again.

Comm II: Attempting to dodge blow. *That still doesn't change the assessment.*

Malraux: First pressing old point, then shifting to the tactic that will win him the battle. *Christmas is coming up. It's very awkward. It's hard enough to find a job when you're healthy. So I thought I'd try something myself ... electric appliance repairs. Their work at Burin Electric is backed up a year sometimes.* Malraux is here suggesting that he has a "sensible" use for the lump sum, and that he has thought through the viability of such a business. Exit Commissioner II, on a mission apparently unrelated to the present case. This precipitous exit has the effect of reducing the significance and credence of Malraux's argument.

Malraux: *$81.56 a month is no good to me.*

Comm I: *You'd like to get established in a small appliance repair?*

Malraux: Emphasizing the soundness of his thought and his business connections. *My father is running Burin Sales, new and second hand furniture, so if we could combine together, it would set me up in more or less what I wanted to do. Any heavy lifting, we'd hire somebody for that.*

Comm I: Pressing for weakness in Malraux's argument. *How much money are you talking about? Do you know?*

Malraux: *You'd have to have a vehicle and a small place of business.* Re-enter Commissioner II. He makes no comment on his absence, emphasizing the insignificance of the hearing.

Comm II: Immediately enters the conversation, embroidering the advantages of pensions. *If you live to age 70, you can draw $31.000.00 out of this.*

Malraux: *What about now?*

Comm II: Strongly, *go to work!*

Malraux: *It's easy to say go to work, but the very first time something goes wrong – say you can't lift something – they resent you.*

Comm II: Attempts two standard strikes, both designed to minimize the perception of Malraux's injury. *Yes, but you've got to find something suitable. If you've lost a leg, you've still got two arms and a leg. There's a man with two legs off in this office right now ...* This opening for the standard ploy of how-well-off-you-are-compared-to-others is squelched by Malraux' reply ...

Malraux: *Harry Wilson?* Indicating that he knows his story and hence blocking the Commissioner from telling the story.

Comm II: *Yes.* Pause. *You're going to lose a lot of money. I'd say $13,000 is your lump sum. A van is five or six thousand.* Implying 'your lump sum would be eaten up quickly and you'd be left with nothing.'

Malraux: Strikes, using free enterprise slogan. *Nothing ventured, nothing gained.* At this point in the drama, it becomes apparent that Malraux has a chance of winning. He is, on the whole, avoiding personalistic arguments, adhering to his demands in a reasonable way (without threats) despite the Commissioner's arguments, and most important, beginning to argue in terms of the WCB values of the work ethic and business initiative.

Comm II: *The Board is very reluctant to pay out lump sums. We've got no guarantee. You've got grade seven, and rehab was talking to you about trades college: get upgraded.* An attempt to return to an alternative theme.

Comm I: *What have you got against upgrading?*

Malraux: Weakly, *it'd take an awful lot of time.*

Comm II: *The government would sponsor you to school. There's lots of jobs you could do, although you may not be able to find any.* A damaging admission. *You could do lots of jobs to keep you going.*

Malraux: *There's lots with a university education can't get work.* Strike.

Comm I: *What do you want us to do? You have no idea how much it's going to cost.* An attack on Malraux' irresponsibility and ignorance of business.

Comm II: *It's your money, but it's our responsibility to make you use it properly.*

Malraux: *I could use whatever the Board would give me.*

Comm II: Pressing argument that Malraux should reconsider, that a lump sum is a big gamble. *We've set aside a $13,000 reserve. You can't get anymore than that.*

Comm I: *You'd like it with no strings, wouldn't you? But if your condition gets worse over the years, it's still our responsibility.*

Malraux: *You wouldn't be obligated if I took a lump sum. I can't pay my bills on $80 a month.*

Comm I: *Compensation isn't designed to pay all your bills.*

Malraux: *Eighty-one dollars is no good to me.* Malraux is not making any headway with the repetition of this point, but it is a useful delaying device until the correct argument is found. *I earned $11,000 last year.*

Comm II: Attacks on bureaucratic grounds. *You said you earned $11,000 last year? There's nothing in your file says that. On your form you said you made $725 a month.* This argument has no point whatever other than to put Malraux back on the defensive.

Malraux: *Eight hundred a month and $2000 baby bonus.*

Comm II: *The form says $725. We go by that.*

Comm I: *The easiest thing in the world for us to do is to commute your pension, but it's not the wisest thing.*

Comm II: Tentative capitulation, giving instructions to Malraux on how to achieve objective. *You've got to have what you want spelt out. Could you get a letter from the manager of Burin electric saying that there may be a place for a business like that?*

Malraux: *Yes.*

Comm II: Confirms possibility of WCB capitulation. *Vince, you come up with a proposition and we may be able to help you, either with a loan or maybe even commute your pension. It's not cut and dried.*

Malraux: *It's going to be a bit difficult to do.* Vagueness suggests current proposition unworkable.

Comm II: *Once you get organized, O.K.*

Exit Malraux.

ACT TWO

Same scene as before, two minutes after Malraux has exited.

Comm I: *See how negative he is! But he'll be back in a week with a proposition for just about $13,000, you watch.*

Comm II: *He's out of work, eh? With that coat and making payments on a new car.* Looking out window, they see Malraux driving off in new large car.

Comm I: *He's been working while drawing TTD, and that's illegal. Mind you* (conversion of negative evaluation to a positive one) *it shows you he wants to make a buck. He's a good opportunist* (that is, his values are congruent with WCB business values). *He's a lot better risk than he'd be if he sat around the last year just drawing compensation.* Justification of WCB intransigence, for themselves and for ethnographer.

Comm II: *He has no idea what he wants the money for.*

Comm I: *He just wants the $13,000. We shouldn't have told him how much he'll get. I wouldn't have told him. He's got a totally closed mind.*

Comm II: (to ethnographer) *We made $700,000 last year on the investment of our reserves. The employers don't want us giving all that money out. We need it. Our administration costs last year were only $800,000.*

Comm I: *Anyway, Canada Pensions'll give you a 100 percent disability pension on top of ours. They don't have any standards like we do. If we've given them* [the disabled workers] *any disability rating at all, they'll* [Canada Pensions Officials] *write them out for 100 percent pensions.*

Comm II: *And if we give them a lump sum, five years later somebody meets him all crippled up, and he'll say, "yes I've lost a leg and I'm getting no compensation." He's not lying, it's what I call the lying truth.*

ACT THREE

Scene: same office, one week later. Malraux is in same seat, armed with a sheaf of bills.

Malraux: *I've changed my mind.*

Comm I: *You want the pension?*

Malraux: *No. I changed my mind about the store. I checked into running the store, and I couldn't guarantee the income.* Once he understood that he would have to account for the funds, he had to find a more realistic proposal.

Comm II: *Then you want the pension?*

Malraux: *No. I want to fix up my longliner. I bought it last spring with my $4300 severance pay. I need a new engine, that's $4200, and a radio telephone, sounder, nets, and gear. It comes to $12,100. Here's the bills. I'm buying 300 lobster pots with another man and we're going lobstering and for salmon in Placentia Bay.*

Comm I: Conceding defeat. *We'll take it to the chairman.*

Exit Malraux.

Comm I: (to ethnographer), *Let's face it, this guy is a winner. He's got it all thought out. He's a go-getter, a self-starter. He'll make it. So we're meeting the chairman this afternoon. We're going to commute his pension and give him the money.*

Comment. After a short flurry of traditionalist personalistic arguments, Malraux concentrated his assault on distinctly non-traditionalist tactics: stubborn argument (a full-fledged traditionalist would have given in to authority earlier); the embrace of WCB business values (the work ethic, the entrepreneurial spirit); and "business-like" organization (the preparation of his case for a longliner). Throughout his first visit, Malraux refused to buckle under the barrage of charges and strikes from the Commissioners, shifting ground when Board tactics held him to an impasse, and seizing his advantage when he saw that his own tactics were weakening the Board.

After Malraux' departure, the Commissioners' act comprised: 1) an attempt to justify their previous intransigence; 2) an expression of hostility at the loss of the battle, 3) justification of the change of decision by converting what had been read as negative cues to positive ones (his dishonesty in working while receiving temporary total pension is transformed into good opportunism).

At Malraux's return visit, the Board, knowing it was defeated, devoted their energies to consolidating their view of Malraux as a "winner," assuring themselves that their capitulation was the correct course.

The case is interesting not only for its intrinsic ethnographic value, but for its illustration of the forces operating in areas of WCB discretion. No discretionary analysis is allowed officials in cases where an industrial disease, such as lung cancer, is unequivocally diagnosed. But when the worker is operating in an area open to the discretion of bureaucrats, the only means by which a worker can obtain his objectives is by rejecting his own cosmology and its logical modes, and embracing that of the WCB.[16] Had Malraux not been the son of an entrepreneur, and himself a foreman, already plucked from the traditionalist mould by the mine hierarchy, and had he not spent years in Toronto in contact with alternative cosmologies, it is unlikely that he would have been able to marshall the behavioural style and logical modes necessary to win "the battle." One suggestion here then is that in non-mechanical WCB decisions, it is the marginal traditionalist who has most chance of success.

Post-Victory Border Skirmishes
Once the disabled miner has "earned" his full pension, his efforts are often devoted to harrassing the WCB. This continual harrassment is partially a function of the assumption that the Board is "out to do us," and unless continually watched, may deprive the pensioners of what is rightfully due them. It is also, if I may say so, a form of sport indulged in by long-term pensioners. Whether it is defense or sport, the form these skirmishes takes is the continued request for clarification of regulations, occasional attempts to dodge these regulations, and the frequent application for types of subsidy which are not provided by the WCB. For example, one miner requested a set of false teeth: "In December I had all my teeth extracted because they were so decayed that they were destroying my health ... I cannot afford to replace them because you know the salary I am getting isn't enough to buy false teeth."

In harrassing the WCB, the primary objective is often to "do" the Board. One miner, who had "fought for years to get Compensation," was finally diagnosed as having silicosis and put on a 100-percent disability pension. In addition, he was entitled to retroactive payment of $5,264.03 for lost work time. Through a clerical error, the WCB issued two cheques valued at $5,264.03 each. When they discovered their error and tried to reclaim one of the cheques, the pensioner claimed that since it was their mistake, he was not obliged to repay them. "Who made this mistake, which to my knowledge was a grave one? *I* did not make this mistake." When the WCB insisted, he moved to a second argument: that he had spent all the money. "When I received this money I was overjoyed so I took my family on a holiday, because realizing I haven't much longer to live, I may never get the chance again." Before capitulating, he resorted to empty threats: "I am telling you whoever it concerns, don't meddle with my Compensation. I shall fight it in a court of law and you may end up paying an extra salary for my deafness and fingers for which I received actually nothing, only $200 monthly on which I actually starved."

Finally, the ailing miners attempt, and almost invariably fail, to bureaucratize, themselves; that is, they try to manipulate regulations in legalistic terms in order to increase the benefits. One such case, after a new amendment to the Act was introduced, aimed at eliminating anomalies in the legislation that sometimes permitted disabled miners to receive less funds than their widows would after their death. (To accomplish this, one disabled miner was paid as if he were a widow, and he was therefore entitled to a series of additional benefits.) Undoubtedly drafted by one of the many St. Lawrence youths that attend Memorial University, the letter attempted to out-bureaucratize the bureaucrats: "Since August 1972, I have been receiving a Compensation pension. At first, my wife and children had to continue receiving Social Assistance. Due to the amendment of the Act, my pension was cut back to Widow Status so that my children could be covered at $50 per child. This, as you can see, left my wife receiving no allowance at all. I fail to see this decision and feel that she must be entitled to some sort of assistance either from the Compensation Board or Social Assistance. Would you kindly investigate this so that it may be clarified and so that I may receive my full entitlement that is due me under the Workmen's Compensation Act?"

In sum, the encounter between disabled miner and the WCB deploy distinctive sets of strikes, blocks, and counters which are derived from their respective cosmologies. The 'pure' traditionalists use threat, personalism, their network of patrons, and prayer in an attempt to accomplish their ends. Most of these, however, are singularly ineffective against the WCB; and it is only when the miner can "shed" his ideology and embrace WCB values that his case can be won in a discretionary situation. In non-discretionary situations, when the claimant's pension is determined entirely by the medical classification of his disease – as is so in the vast majority of St. Lawrence cases – the encounter, with the personalist pleas of the traditionalist, is foredoomed. Here the function of the encounter is not to re-evaluate a case, but to convince the miner of the legitimacy of the WCB's decision. From the miner's perspective then, the encounter is a dance of irrelevance.

IRRATIONAL RATIONALITY

The energies of this essay have been directed towards demonstrating what is axiomatic in anthropology – that rationality, like beauty, lies in the eye of the beholder. Throughout the industrial world, bureaucracy is widely conceived of as the ultimate social mechanism for the rational and efficient administration of social and economic policies. This conception of bureaucracy is based as much on the vulgarization of Weberian thought as it is on the empirical observation of these monoliths' activities. As I have already remarked in the preamble to this essay, Weber's theoretical assessment of an ideal construct has entered the popular language of industrial social thought as a scientific statement of actual virtue. If it is difficult to live in the modern world without frequent exposure to evidence that belittles bureaucracy's rationality, a simple belief in bureaucracy's potential superiority is, nevertheless, one of the gentle delusions of our time.

But no such gentility informs the clash between the Workmen's Compensation Board and the communities of St. Lawrence and Lawn. Here, an administrative machine created to indemnify the disabled and the suffering does so at stunning cost to the communities. This social cost is a function of neither "over-organization" nor of "nepotism, favoritism, graft [and] corruption" (Merton *et al*, 1952:396). Rather, it is a function of the bureaucracy's incompatibility with traditionalist logical and social modes. It is so because the bureaucratic logic violates fundamental traditionalist conceptions and principles. One set of violated traditionalist notions is the expectations *vis-à-vis* confrontation and argument. The disparate notions held by bureaucrat and traditionalist to regulate interaction are such that a true universe of discourse – of the exchange of information and the acceptance of shared constraints – is impossible.

A second set of violated traditionalist notions are those regarding just restitution. Here there are three zones of incompatibility. The first is the use of different criteria in the *classification of disease*: for the traditionalists there is simply "the mine disease," whereas the bureaucrats distinguish between cancers, heart diseases, silicosis, and the whole range of disorders classified loosely under the heading of chronic obstructive pulmonary diseases. The perception of the *cause of disease* is also conflicting: the traditionalists see work in the mine as the cause of all health disorders, whereas the bureaucrats insist that it is often impossible to determine if a disease has an industrial cause. Finally, their perception of *just compensation* is at variance, for the traditionalists believe that all sufferers from the mine disease are entitled to compensation without enduring the stigma of welfare; the bureaucrats, on the other hand, insist that fine distinctions be made (by disease and by degree of impairment) in the disbursement of WCB monies. Thus traditionalist egality embraces economic disability and rejects the bureaucratic egality in their "artificial" scientific distinctions. Traditionalist rationality insists that cause and effect are obvious (mine = industrial disease), and rejects the bureaucratic rationality that society should 'reward' a cancer and 'punish' a heart disease.

Unfortunately for the people of St. Lawrence and Lawn, their lives are inextricably intertwined with an alien social form which appears to systematically contradict their fundamental moral and cognitive principles. It remains to be seen whether this is an inescapable characteristic of bureaucracy when dealing with a traditional sector of society, or whether such contradictions can be overridden by a humane determination. What has certainly been established in this essay is that a bureaucracy attempting to rationally alleviate suffering in a social disaster must refrain from composing its regulations in a social vacuum, in a closed logical system, that does not take into account the perceptions and principles of the suffering population.

NOTES

1 Keith Matthews, personal communication.
2 Due to inadequate diagnoses, precise figures on mine-linked deaths will never be known. Neither can a definitive figure be given for the number of presently disabled miners, as considerable controversy still surrounds the interpretation and compensation of industrial disease.
3 Local usage, meaning medically certified as unable to work.
4 I am grateful indeed to a member of the Board, Mr. Richard A. Fagan, for guiding me through the complexities of the Act.
5 This seems to be a matter of debate in medical circles.
6 My earlier book on St. Lawrence, *Dying Hard*, was exclusively a compendium of traditionalistic perspectives. Some of the cases presented below are from *Dying Hard*, permitting any bewildered reader of the previous book to extrapolate the WCB's rationale here.
7 The quotes in this section and in all descriptions of the bureaucratic perception are from WCB documents or interviews. They have been edited.
8 I am indebted to Professor Ronald Schwartz for this observation. Cf. also Schwartz (1974).
9 A case could certainly be made for the miners' rude empiricism which has probably been more accurate than the scientists' regarding diagnosis, prognosis, and treatment.
10 The recipient of this letter can neither read nor write.
11 Some men do obtain other jobs, either in "surface work" with the same company, or in another firm. Their partial disability pension is a supplement to their salary, and they bear no short-term socio-economic burden.
12 Of the 74 disabled miners who are still living, only 17 are classed as '100-percenters'; the majority (69% of pensioners) have received ratings from 30% to 60% disability).
13 I am indebted to various WCB medical and administrative officials who guided me in the analysis which follows. As WCB intellectuals, their perception of the dilemmas of public policy are as astute as any analyst's. Special thanks to Dr. W. E. Lawton of the WCB Medical Division, Messrs William May, Andrew Rose, and Richard Fagan of the Board; and Messrs Max Bursey and John Bambrick of the Claims Division. Some of the cases presented are composites, some are verbatim transcriptions; in all of them, situations and participants are disguised.
14 This low rate of compensation prevalent at that time has now been increased.
15 This conclusion should not be entirely dismissed. Manning's M.H.A. and patron is a powerful member of the present cabinet, and undoubtedly was instrumental in changing WCB regulations.
16 WCB officials, of course, miss the ironic fact that in attempting to squeeze more money out of the Board, disabled miners are in fact embracing the work ethic – especially since they see a 100-percent disability pension as the just reward for their laborious battle with the Board.

APPENDIX

REPORT TO THE PREMIER OF NEWFOUNDLAND, 1976
Elliott Leyton

Note: The recommendations which follow were submitted to the Premier of Newfoundland in July of 1976, together with a draft of the "*Bureaucratization of Anguish*" (this vol.).

A. INTRODUCTION

One need only leaf through any of the autobiographies in *Dying Hard* to understand that the WCB, designed to alleviate anguish among the distressed people of St. Lawrence, has in fact caused a great deal of anguish on its own. The explanation for this apparent paradox lies not in any ill intent but in sociological forces which distort the impact of government and WCB on the affected communities.

First, the Workmen's Compensation Act is not an integrated piece of legislation. The Act, with its many amendments, is a piecemeal attempt to patch up obvious deficiencies in its coverage, without fully understanding the impact of these regulations on the suffering communities, and without understanding that each change in the Act produces unintended consequences (especially that for each new class of person brought under the Act, another similar group is excluded).

Second, by its very nature, the Act imposes bureaucratic – that is, formal and impersonal – criteria on rural and traditional communities which think primarily in terms of personal and functional criteria. For example, "scientific" classifications of 65% disabilities are meaningless in a community where "either you're disabled or you're not." Thus terrible bitterness is generated by what the people of St. Lawrence and Lawn see as fundamentally unfair and unequal treatment of disabled miners and widows by the Board.

Third, Workmen's Compensation Boards may have been established throughout the industrial world to remove the disabled worker and his employer from an adversary relationship. However, this has merely shifted the adversary relationship to the disabled worker vs. the Board. This reality assaults the philosophy on which Compensation is based: to ignore it is to perpetuate the cycle of struggle and humiliation which traps disabled workers.

B. GENERAL RECOMMENDATIONS

Preamble. Throughout the industrial world, Workmen's Compensation was designed to recompense individual workers for time and money lost through industrial accidents. It was not designed for industrial disease, and it was not designed to handle whole communities that would be devastated by industrial disease. Since this province must brace itself not only for the task of improving conditions in the St. Lawrence area, but also for the possibility of comparable future suffering in other mining centres, it is essential that compensation procedures be fundamentally re-thought.

RECOMMENDATION ONE: IMMEDIATE DEMANDS SHOULD BE MADE THAT THE FEDERAL AND OTHER PROVINCIAL GOVERNMENTS FORM A CENTRAL NATIONAL POOL OF ALL PROVINCIAL WORKMEN'S COMPENSATION BOARDS' DISASTER FUNDS. Newfoundland, a small and poor province, may have as many as three major disasters to support within 15 years, whereas B.C. has none, and Quebec and Ontario but one or two each. Newfoundland cannot afford to support with humanity these staggering costs. Ottawa is doubly obliged to assist in this regard, since the lack of early intervention by the Federal Departments of Health and Mines has contributed materially to the severity of these disasters.

RECOMMENDATION TWO: LEGISLATION SHOULD BE ENACTED DESIGNATING AREAS SUCH AS ST. LAWRENCE AND BAIE VERTE AS SPECIAL PROGRAMME AREAS AND AREAS SO DESIGNATED SHOULD BE TREATED BY A SEPARATE SET OF COMPENSATION REGULATIONS. Legislation which may be adequate, even generous, for an individual worker temporarily incapacitated by industrial accident, is stunningly inadequate for devastated communities.

RECOMMENDATION THREE: SPECIAL AREA COMPENSATION LEGISLATION SHOULD INCLUDE ECONOMIC-FUNCTIONAL ASSESSMENTS OF DISABILITY, NOT BE CONFINED TO ARBITRARY MEDICAL RATINGS. That is, the worker who can no longer work should be classed as 100% disabled and entitled to a full pension, regardless of the precise degree of medical impairment. Failure to do so is to operate against the principle, established in 1958 by the American Medical Association, that "the physician is only competent to evaluate the physical impairment; evaluation of 'disability' is an administrative or judicial function."

RECOMMENDATION FOUR: SPECIAL AREA COMPENSATION LEGISLATION SHOULD AIM AT ELIMINATING THE INFINITY OF DISTINCTIONS BETWEEN PENSIONS AND WORK TO-

WARDS ONE BASIC PENSION. At present, the inequalities of disability classifications and pensions create extraordinary bitterness between families, and go far towards destroying communities. (This applies primarily, of course, to Permanent Partial Pensions.)

RECOMMENDATION FIVE: SPECIAL AREA COMPENSATION LEGISLATION SHOULD ALWAYS BE MORE THAN COMPARABLE WELFARE BENEFITS. Under no circumstances should a disabled worker be forced to endure the stigma of accepting Welfare; nor should his family be forced to enter the Welfare cycle of humiliation and dependence. Nor should he be worth more dead than alive, as he may be under present regulations – as when a "sixty percenter" receiving a partial pension dies of his industrial disease.

RECOMMENDATION SIX: SPECIAL AREA COMPENSATION LEGISLATION MUST PROVIDE NOT JUST INDIVIDUAL PENSIONS, BUT A WHOLE RANGE OF SOCIAL AND ECONOMIC SUPPORT, INCLUDING:
a. Physical support items such as breathing apparatuses and special beds, which are *normally* used in the UK, and would alleviate much suffering.
b. Psychiatric counselling for the anxiety-ridden newly-diagnosed, and the bereaved.
c. Economic alternatives, such as the employment of the partially disabled and widows, and the training of the disabled, widows and orphans (see recommendations for the Rehabilitation Division).
d. Social and recreational facilities for the disabled, including a clubhouse with a social director, and a driver with a van to transport the disabled.

RECOMMENDATION SEVEN: SPECIAL AREA COMPENSATION LEGISLATION SHOULD PROVIDE NOT JUST FOR WORKERS BUT FOR ANY COMMUNITY RESIDENT WHOSE HEALTH IS DAMAGED BY THE INDUSTRY. An industry is responsible for the health of all whose lives it may damage, not just workers.

RECOMMENDATION EIGHT: SPECIAL AREA COMPENSATION LEGISLATION MUST INCLUDE PUNITIVE CLAUSES FOR INDUSTRIES WHICH CAN BE PROVEN TO HAVE WILFULLY IGNORED HEALTH AND SAFETY STANDARDS.

RECOMMENDATION NINE: ALL SPA PENSIONS, PARTIAL OR

TOTAL, TEMPORARY OR PERMANENT, MUST BE INDEXED TO THE COST OF LIVING.

RECOMMENDATION TEN: IN SPA COMMUNITIES, THE BURDEN OF PROOF THAT A DISEASE IS INDUSTRIALLY CAUSED MUST BE SHIFTED FROM THE WORKER TO THE WORKMEN'S COMPENSATION BOARD. Workers should not continue to be penalized for deficiencies in the state of medical research: the current omission of heart failure brought on by chronic obstructive pulmonary disease may be especially anomalous.

RECOMMENDATION ELEVEN: PAIN AND SUFFERING MUST BE MADE COMPENSABLE. While this condition is difficult to evaluate objectively, its omission is inhumane, and I believe that other Canadian provinces provide for it.

RECOMMENDATION TWELVE: THE CASH VALUE OF ALL PENSIONS SHOULD BE GEARED MORE CLOSELY TO WHAT THE DISABLED WOULD HAVE EARNED IF THEY HAD CONTINUED WORKING. At present, men with very large families receive large pensions, while those with small families are badly treated. Further, while total pensions are generous, *only 20% of St. Lawrence miners disabled by disease and accident actually receive total pensions.*

C. THE WCB'S ASSESSMENT DIVISION

Preamble. Although the WCB is in general a smoothly functioning administrative machine, it occupies an ambiguous position in society with its financial responsibility to industry and its legal responsibility to government. This creates an undesirable situation of potentially conflicting loyalties. The WCB is no slave of industry, but it is under continuous pressure from industry and its lobbyists to be "more independent of government" (i.e., to be more dependent on industry). Propriety demands that the WCB be independent of both party politics and industry, and structures should be continually revised to maximize this independence.

RECOMMENDATION THIRTEEN: AS A STEP TOWARDS MAXIMIZING THE INDEPENDENCE OF THE WCB, THE ASSESSMENT DIVISION SHOULD BE SEPARATED FROM THE WCB AND MADE A PART OF GOVERNMENT. That is, the WCB should be indirectly (not directly) financed by industry. Present personnel should be transferred to government employment.

RECOMMENDATION FOURTEEN: THE PRESENT METHODS OF ASSESSING INDUSTRIES WITH SHORT-TERM LOW RISKS BUT LONG-TERM HIGH RISKS ARE UNACCEPTABLE. At present, for example, the asbestos industry receives a very low assessment because it has a low accident rating. It is, however, well known that it takes from 15 to 25 years for asbestos diseases to begin to appear. By this time the asbestos industry may have left the province without having made any substantial contribution to the WCB's Disaster Reserve, leaving the province with an immense liability.

RECOMMENDATION FIFTEEN: ALL EMPLOYERS AND EMPLOYEES IN THE PROVINCE SHOULD BE COVERED BY WCB BENEFITS. The current practice of not covering certain firms, such as small taxi outfits, is iniquitous.

D. THE WCB'S REHABILITATION SECTION

Preamble. The philosophy on which all Canadian Compensation Boards are based – the notion of *indemnification* of workers for lost monies – is quite obsolete and corrosive to the dignity of both worker and society. The philosophy should shift from indemnification to speedy reintegration of the worker into the economy, permitting him to maintain himself and his family with dignity. Members of the WCB complain, quite correctly, that industries are unwilling to cooperate in rehabilitation; but the WCB spends virtually nothing on rehabilitative efforts, and rehabilitation is a *right*, not a privilege dependent on the largesse of employers.

RECOMMENDATION SIXTEEN: ALL REHABILITATION SERVICES IN THE PROVINCE SHOULD BE MERGED INTO ONE POWERFUL CENTRAL AGENCY. At present, they are scattered among many agencies whose efforts are unintegrated, inadequate, and impotent.

RECOMMENDATION SEVENTEEN: THE WCB SHOULD PAY A SUBSTANTIAL PORTION OF ITS INCOME TO THE MAINTENANCE OF THIS NEW CENTRALIZED REHABILITATION AGENCY. The WCB's present expenditure of less than 1% of its total revenue on Rehabilitation is an indication of its current malaise (for example, no rehabilitation effort of any kind has *ever* been directed towards a diseased St. Lawrence miner).

RECOMMENDATION EIGHTEEN: REHABILITATION EFFORTS SHOULD BE AUTOMATIC, NOT DEPENDENT ON WORKERS'

REQUESTS, AND SHOULD INCLUDE NOT ONLY VOCA-
TIONAL RETRAINING BUT PSYCHOLOGICAL COUNSEL-
LING. At present, few are rehabilitated but many are left in anxiety and
ignorance about their disability.

RECOMMENDATION NINETEEN: A PORTION OF WCB FUNDS
SHOULD BE EARMARKED FOR THE ESTABLISHMENT OF
SMALL LOCAL INDUSTRIES FOR THE DISABLED, AS THE
BRITISH RE-EMPLOY SYSTEM HAS BEEN DOING FOR YEARS.
The government should reconsider its advice from civil servants and
economists who long ago worked out all the reasons why nothing can
even be done, and resigned themselves to it. In this regard, the control of
markets is perhaps more critical than productive capacity.

RECOMMENDATION TWENTY: REHABILITATION WORKERS
MUST BE TRAINED PROFESSIONALS. This necessarily entails
proper salaries, proper university training, and increased powers (in the
present malaise, WCB training consists of one week spent reading the
Compensation Act, and powers are as trivial as driving around the island
distributing incontinence pads).

E. THE WCB'S SAFETY SECTION

Preamble. Like the Rehabilitation section, personnel of the Safety Division
are treated in an unprofessional manner; badly paid, poorly trained, and
given very limited powers. Despite this inadequate training (most are
tradesmen who know very little, for example, about industrial disease) and
limited power (the fines levied are trivial), they have the awesome responsibility for all non-mine safety and hygiene in the province. Further, they
are often intimidated since they are enjoined to monitor the safety and
health conditions of industries which pay their salaries.

Worse still, as throughout this country, the responsibility for health and
safety is divided among a morass of overlapping and conflicting Federal and
Provincial agencies – including the Department of Mines, Labour, Health,
Environment, and the WCB – whose record of performance is exceedingly
inadequate (St. Lawrence, Baie Verte, Cape Breton, Thetford Mines, Elliot
Lake, to name a few).

RECOMMENDATION TWENTY-ONE: THE RESPONSIBILITY
FOR INDUSTRIAL SAFETY AND HYGIENE SHOULD BE RE-
MOVED FROM THE WCB, AND THE FUNDS RELEASED FOR
THE ESTABLISHMENT OF A POWERFUL CENTRALIZED
PROVINCIAL AGENCY RESPONSIBLE FOR ALL SAFETY AND

HYGIENE IN THE PROVINCE. Present personnel should be transferred to the safety (not hygiene) section of this new agency.

RECOMMENDATION TWENTY-TWO: THE NEW AGENCY SHOULD BE GIVEN SWEEPING POWERS AND PROVIDED WITH TRAINED PROFESSIONAL PERSONNEL. The agency personnel should be enforcing the regulations within the province, as well as keeping abreast properly of all developments in leading nations (such as the UK).

RECOMMENDATION TWENTY-THREE: THE PHILOSOPHY OF THE NEW AGENCY SHOULD BE BASED ON AN EXPLICIT RECOGNITION OF THE CHAOS OF CURRENT CANADIAN REGULATIONS. The unreliability of the Federal Departments has been amply illustrated in the five-year delay in the health investigation at St. Lawrence (see the 1969 Royal Commission), and the more recent full year spent in "analysing" data from Baie Verte.

F. THE WCB'S BOARD, CLAIMS, AND PENSIONS DIVISIONS

Preamble. These are extremely competent operations, but their sensitive nature exposes them to special problems which should be recognized and dealt with. One problem is the unhealthy structural position of the WCB *vis-à-vis* industry, which prompted one WCB official to remark to me, "after all, that's who we have to answer to." Such a dependence relationship, ideological or otherwise, is insidious and should be avoided.

A second problem has to do with the attitudes of WCB officials to the people of the St. Lawrence area. The essentially adversary relationship between worker and WCB naturally enough creates hurt feelings among some WCB staff who feel that their efforts to help the workers are unappreciated. Most WCB officials are sensitive enough to overlook this. But some retreat into an ugly pseudo-racism which defines the people of St. Lawrence as "people with no initiative," even genetically inferior. Regardless, whether sensitive or angered, in neither case is there usually a clear understanding of the social and cultural factors which make people of the St. Lawrence area behave as they do *vis-à-vis* the WCB. This lack of understanding has destructive consequences for individuals and communities.

RECOMMENDATION TWENTY-FOUR: RECRUITMENT TO ALL LEVELS OF THE WCB, BUT MOST ESPECIALLY THE BOARD ITSELF, MUST BE KEPT FREE OF BOTH POLITICAL PATRONAGE AND AN UNBALANCED INDUSTRIAL VOICE. The Conservative government's rejection of the Liberal patronage principle is laud-able, but it should be reinforced by continued recruitment to the Board from (a) the elite members of the Claims Division, who deal with all these critical issues, and (b) representatives of Labour (such as a prominent union leader) as well as local businessmen.

RECOMMENDATION TWENTY-FIVE: WCB OFFICIALS (IN-DEED, ALL GOVERNMENT OFFICIALS) WHO DEAL WITH THE PUBLIC, EITHER FACE TO FACE OR BY LETTER, SHOULD BE SENSITIZED (POSSIBLY THROUGH A SPECIALLY DESIGNED UNIVERSITY COURSE) TO SEVERAL FUNDAMENTAL SO-CIAL ISSUES, INCLUDING:

(a) People of certain areas of this province are neither genetically nor behaviourally inferior.
(b) The behaviour of those who are caught in an industrial disaster (or in any tragedy) is a consequence of social and cultural forces to which all humans are subject.
(c) That all levels of society should be treated with respect, not "re-spectfully request" to employers and "you will report ..." to employees.
(d) There are special problems encountered in communicating bureau-cratic regulations to relatively uneducated workers, and special techniques must be developed for this.

G. LIAISON OF THE WCB WITH OTHER AGENCIES

Preamble. At the moment, aside from the exchange of pension information between the WCB and the Department of Social Assistance, there is very little coordination between efforts of the various provincial and federal Departments. The consequence of this is always unfortunate.

RECOMMENDATION TWENTY-SIX: THE GOVERNMENT SHOULD LEGISLATE THAT, FOR THE PURPOSE OF THE DE-PARTMENT OF SOCIAL ASSISTANCE, WCB PERMANENT PARTIAL DISABILITY PENSIONS BE TREATED AS INCOME NOT AS PENSIONS. At the moment, St. Lawrence people with per-manent partial disability pensions of, say $100 a month, who are unable to work find their $100 automatically deducted from their Welfare.

RECOMMENDATION TWENTY-SEVEN: THE GOVERNMENT SHOULD CONSIDER LAUNCHING LEGAL ACTION AGAINST CORPORATIONS WHOSE ACTIVITIES IN THE PROVINCE HAVE DAMAGED THE HEALTH OF WORKERS.

RECOMMENDATION TWENTY-EIGHT: THE GOVERNMENT SHOULD CONSIDER THE LONG-TERM INEVITABILITY OF ELIMINATING THE WCB. The WCB is essentially an anachronism of an immature civilization; for a mature civilization will pension a totally disabled household head, re-train a partially disabled worker and reintegrate him into society, without regard to whether his/her disability occurred on the job.

RECOMMENDATION TWENTY-NINE: THE GOVERNMENT SHOULD RECOGNIZE THAT MEMORIAL UNIVERSITY CONTAINS SCHOLARS WITH EXPERTISE RELEVANT TO PRACTICAL PROBLEMS. This recognition could take two forms:

(a) The provision of a course (as in recommendation 25) on the social relationship between public servant and client: this should be required for public servants in compensation, rehabilitiation, welfare, courts and corrections.
(b) That the anthropological/sociological evaluation of departments, such as this report, be made a more routine part of government operations. Such social perspectives provide useful insights, I believe, into unnecessary strains in otherwise smoothly functioning organizations. They are also free.

Conclusion

Elliott Leyton

4

Both essays in this volume concentrate on the one institutional form which has come to dominate social life in industrial societies. More specifically, the essays deal with the logic by which bureaucrats operate in their encounters with their clients in island Newfoundland. Here, because of high unemployment, the population has been especially dependent upon the largesse of various government agencies, thanks to the recent history of Newfoundland – the superimposition of large federally funded bureaucracies on a decaying, primary-resource economy (cf. Alexander, 1977). In the small and personalistic world of Newfoundlanders, the operations of bureaucracies are highly visible and pertinent to the lives of many. This does not mean of course that bureaucracy is structurally more significant in such a society than it would be elsewhere; for bureaucracy is *the* organizing principle of modern society, and its powers continually encroach on spheres regulated by more traditional institutions such as the family and the community.

Whereas the authors' congruence of interest gives this volume both focus and coherence, we hope, this should not be allowed to obscure the differences in aim and theoretical approach that distinguish the essays from one another. Theoretically, both essays begin with Max Weber (as must any explication of bureaucracy). Handelman's essay concentrates on the "stock of knowlege" held by the official and the process by which the perception of specific cases is altered and shaped by this knowledge. In the application of rule to case, the official must add his/her officially uncodified "common-sense" assumptions about the motivation and character of the client in order to decide what "really happened." But in an important way, what really happened was the imposition of a differential credence on information provided by people in different social positions, and the use of precedent and experience, as well as of future projections in determining the "facts" of the present. To use Handelman's encapsulation, "the application of rule to case, in Weber's terms, passes through a landscape of assumptions and interpretations that ostensibly have little to do with the journey, but that on closer examination, are found to constitute the journey itself." Essentially then, Handelman's theoretical position is a phenomenological one, which "assumes the bureaucratic life-world to be an arbitrary but integrated and meaningful social construct"; and he uses his data in order to enrich our understanding of the dynamics which enable the bureaucratic world to function.

My own essay also takes its starting point from Max Weber, but its explicit theoretical concern is not to enrich the Weberian model. Rather, it is to dwell on the negative and dysfunctional aspects of bureaucracy – aspects which have been ignored or misunderstood by many of Weber's intellectual descendants. From my own point of view, bureaucracy's evils stem not from "over- or under-organization," but from its dual position as enforcer of order on behalf of the industrial power structure (be it capitalist or socialist), and as creator of a depersonalized view of the world often incompatible with humane social life. Together, these positions produce a universe of discord. Thus the WCB, charged with the responsibility of indemnifying diseased workers and their families, is restrained in two ways from fulfilling its obligations. First, its ultimate dependence on industry and the work ethic compel it to function in a manner which is frequently not in the interests of the workers; and secondly, the conflicting assumptions of logic and values implicit in the bureaucrat's and traditionalist's world views (assumptions about the nature of egality, scientific proof, and moral legitimacy) have shaped a milieu in which the majority of recipients feel alienated and betrayed. Thus, whereas perhaps one-fifth of the diseased workers receive full pensions and are able to maintain their position in society as long as they live, the remainder are subject to the centrifugal forces which degrade the status of worker and widow, and spin apart kin and community.

This brings me to a second difference between the essays. Handelman's goal (and his achievement) is to enrich social science, and in the process of doing so, he often illuminates issues of wider social concern. My own perspective (however outdated it may be) is that of the social reformer: my concern is with the social issues themselves, although I hope that, in passing, I make a contribution to academic social science as well.

The consequences of these differing priorities, however, are less in the kinds of analysis employed than in the specific bureaucracies chosen for study. Those whose concern is reform are more likely to select a bureaucracy whose activities have clearly negative consequences for the people whose lives they touch – rather than the many social agencies which simply make the best of a difficult task. An additional consequence of these differing priorities is that the academic whose concern is reform is often obliged to go one step beyond pure analytic reportage and step into the practical world of specific recommendations for change. Government officials frequently complain, with justification, that the customary withering scorn of academics is quite useless to them. Hence, to be effective, the academic must be prepared to sally into the real world, at least to the point where he can present a more humane blueprint for the institution he has studied. (The Appendix at the end of my essay contains my own attempt to do so for the WCB.) Although this step is no guarantee of success, to ignore it is to ensure inaction: the most effective technique of all, however, is to make the recommendations part of the platform of a political action group.

Whichever role the anthropologist cares to adopt, the importance of the study of bureaucracy should be readily apparent. The impact of bureaucracy is in some ways more intense in Canada than in other industrial nations (its unemployment rate and welfare rolls are among the highest in the world, as is the proportion of its population in prisons). But each nation has its distinctive organizational characteristics, and none can be free from bureaucratic ones, since the bureaucratic mode of organization is fundamental to the structure of the modern state. Why, then, are bureaucratic premises and behaviours antithetical to many human values? To answer this question, it is necessary to analyse these centres of power, wherever they may reign in the modern world.

None of this social concern would be effective without the necessary spadework performed by the purely intellectual exploration of these institutions. Handelman's ethnography is filled with insights into the bureaucratic decision-making process, insights through which our understanding of the bureaucratic world is enriched. In dealing with the dilemmas, the contradictions, the pressures, the ambiguity, the host of subtle and sometimes conflicting cues which the case worker must make meaningful, Handelman does far more than merely illuminate the encounter between bureaucrat and client. What he succeeds in doing is making the bureaucrat human, reacting as we would all react to intense and contradictory pressures. This act of making the participants of another sub-culture or institution fully human is, and must always be, the central task of anthropology.

References

ALEXANDER, D.
1977 *The Decay of Trade: An Economic History of the Newfoundland Saltfish Trade*, 1935–1965. St. John's Institute of Social and Economic Research, Memorial University of Newfoundland.

ARONOFF, M.
1974 *Frontiertown: the Politics of Community Building in Israel*. Manchester, Manchester University Press.

BALDWIN, E.
1972 *Differentiation and Co-operation in an Israeli Veteran Moshav*. Manchester, Manchester University Press.

BERREMAN, G.
1974 "Bringing it all Back Home: Malaise in Anthropology." In Dell Hymes (ed.), *Reinventing Anthropology*. New York, Vintage Books.

BITTNER, EGON
1965 "The Concept of Organization." *Social Research*, 32:230–55.

BITTNER, EGON
1967 "The Police on Skid Row: a Study in Peace Keeping." *American Sociological Review*, 32:701–6.

BITTNER, EGON
1973 "Objectivity and Realism in Sociology." In George Psathas (ed.), *Phenomenological Sociology*. New York, John Wiley.

BLAU, PETER M.
1956 *Bureaucracy in Modern Society*. New York, Random House.

BLAU, PETER M. and MARSHALL METER
1971 *Bureacracy in Modern Society*. Second Edition. New York, Random House.

BLUM, ALAN F. and PETER McHUGH
1971 "The Social Ascription of Motives." *American Sociological Review*, 36:98–109.

BLUMBERG, ABRAHAM
1970 *Criminal Justice*. Chicago, Quadrangle Books.

BOISSEVAIN, JEREMY
1974 *Friends of Friends*. Oxford, Basil Blackwell.

CHIARAMONTE, LOUIS J.
1970 *Craftsman-Client Contracts: Interpersonal Relations in a Newfoundland Fishing Community*. St. John's, Institute of Social and Economic Research, Memorial University of Newfoundland.

CICOUREL, AARON
1968 *The Social Organization of Juvenile Justice*. New York, John Wiley.

CICOUREL, AARON
1973 *Cognitive Sociology*. Harmondsworth, Penguin Books.

DAVOREN, E.
1974 "The Role of the Social Worker." In Ray Helfer and Henry Kempe (eds.), *The Battered Child* (second edition). Chicago, University of Chicago Press.

EMERSON, ROBERT M.
1969 *Judging Delinquents: Context and Process in Juvenile Court*. Chicago, Aldine.
EPSTEIN, DAVID G.
1972 "The Genesis and Function of Squatter Settlements in Brasilia." In Thomas Weaver and Douglas Whites (eds.), *The Anthropology of Urban Environments*. Boulder, The Society for Applied Anthropology.
FALLERS, LLOYD A.
1965 *Bantu Bureaucracy*. Chicago, University of Chicago Press.
FARIS, J. C.
1972 *Cat Harbour: A Newfoundland Fishing Settlement*. St. John's, Institute of Social and Economic Research, Memorial University of Newfoundland.
FEDERAL-PROVINCIAL STUDY GROUP ON ALIENATION
1974 Report. Ottawa, Mimeo.
FRIED, MORTON H.
1967 *The Evolution of Political Society*. New York, Random House.
GARFINKEL, HAROLD
1967 *Studies in Ethnomethodology*. Englewood Cliffs, N.J., Prentice Hall.
GEERTZ, CLIFFORD
1973 "Politics Past, Politics Present: Some Notes on the Use of Anthropology in Understanding the New States." In *The Interpretation of Cultures*. New York, Basic Books.
GELLES, RICHARD J.
1974 "Child Abuse as Psychopathology: a Sociological Critique and Reformulation." In Suzanne Steinmetz and Murray Strauss (eds.), *Violence in the Family*. New York, Dodd, Mead.
GIL, DAVID G.
1973 *Violence Against Children: Physical Child Abuse in the United States*. Boston, Harvard University Press.
GLUCKMAN, MAX
1968 "Inter-hierarchical roles: Professional and Party Ethics in Tribal Areas in South and Central Africa." In M. Swartz (ed.), *Local Level Politics*. Chicago, Aldine.
GREENAWAY, W. K.
1973 "Faith and Science in the Professional Ideology of Social Caseworkers: 'Vocabularies of Motives' and Results." Paper read to the Atlantic Association of Anthropologists and Sociologists.
GRILLO, RALPH D.
1973 *African Railwaymen*. Cambridge, Cambridge University Press.
HANDELMAN, DON
1971 "Patterns of Interaction in a Sheltered Workship in Jerusalem." University of Manchester, Unpublished Ph.D. thesis.
HANDELMAN, DON
1976 "Bureaucratic Transactions: the Development of Official-Client Relationships." In Bruce Kapferer (ed.), *Transaction and Meaning: Directions in the Anthropology of Exchange and Symbolic Behavior*. Philadelphia, Institute for the Study of Human Issues.
HANDELMAN, DON
n.d. "Bureaucratic Affiliation: The Moral Component in Welfare Instances from Urban Israel."
HELFER, RAY. E.
1974 "The Responsibility and Role of the Physician." In Ray Helfer and Henry Kempe (eds.), *The Battered Child* (second edition). Chicago, University of Chicago Press.

HYMES, DELL
1974 "The Use of Anthropology: Critical, Political, Personal." In Dell Hymes (ed.), *Reinventing Anthropology*. New York, Vintage Books.
JAY, ROBERT R.
1969 *Javanese Villagers*. Boston, MIT Press.
JEHENSON, ROGER
1973 "A Phenomenological Approach to the Study of the Formal Organization." In George Psathas (ed.), *Phenomenological Sociology*. New York, John Wiley.
KAPFERER, BRUCE
1972 *Strategy and Transaction in an African Factory*. Manchester, Manchester University Press.
KAY, HERMA H.
1969 "The Offer of a Free Home: a Case Study in the Family Law of the Poor." In Laura Nader (ed.), *Law in Culture and Society*. Chicago, Aldine.
KEMPE, HENRY ET AL.
1962 "The Battered-Child Syndrome." *Journal of the American Medical Association*, 181:17–24.
KESSLER, H. H.
1970 *Disability – Determination and Evaluation*. Philadelphia, Lea and Febiger.
KIEFER, CHRISTIE W.
1970 "The Psychological Interdependence of Family, School, and Bureaucracy in Japan." *American Anthropologist*, 72:66–75.
KUSHNER, GILBERT
1970 "The Anthropology of Complex Societies." In Bernard J. Siegel (ed.), *Biennial Review of Anthropology*, 1969. Stanford, Stanford University Press.
LEE, DOROTHY
1950 "Lineal and Nonlineal Codifications of Reality." *Psychosomatic Medicine*, 12:89–97.
LEEDS, ANTHONY
1973 "Locality Power in Relation to Supralocal Power Institutions." In Aidan Southall (ed.), *Urban Anthropology*. New York, Oxford.
LEYTON, ELLIOTT (ed.)
1974 *The Compact: Selected Dimensions of Friendship*. St. John's, Institute of Social and Economic Research, Memorial University of Newfoundland.
LEYTON, ELLIOTT
1975 *Dying Hard: the Ravages of Industrial Carnage*. Toronto, McClelland and Stewart.
LING, KEN
1972 *The Revenge of Heaven*. New York, Ballantine.
MARX, EMANUEL
1973 "Coercive Violence in Official-client Relationships." *Israel Studies in Criminology*, 2:33–68.
MERTON, ROBERT K. et al. (eds.)
1952 *Reader in Bureaucracy*. Glencoe, Ill., The Free Press.
MORRIS, MARIAN G. AND ROBERT W. GOULD
1963 "Role Reversal: a Concept in Dealing with the Neglected/Battered-Child Syndrome." In *The Neglected Battered-Child Syndrome*. New York, Child Welfare League of America.
MOUZELIS, NICOS
1969 *Organisation and Bureaucracy*. Chicago, Aldine.
NADER, LAURA
1974 "Up the Anthropologist – Perspectives Gained from Studying Up." In Dell Hymes (ed.), *Reinventing Anthropology*. New York, Vintage Books.

NEMEC, THOMAS

1976 "The History, Ecology and Organization of an Anglo-Irish-Newfoundland Outport Fishery." University of Michigan, Unpublished Ph.D. Dissertation.

PAINE, ROBERT

1975 "An Exploratory Analysis in 'Middle-class' culture." In Elliott Leyton (ed.), *The Compact: Selected Dimensions of Friendship*. St. John's, Institute of Social and Economic Research, Memorial University of Newfoundland.

PAULSEN, M. G.

1974 "The Law and Abused Children." In Ray Helfer and Henry Kempe (eds.), *The Battered Child* (second edition). Chicago, University of Chicago Press.

PLATT, ANTHONY M.

1969 *The Child Savers: the Invention of Delinquency*. Chicago, University of Chicago Press.

POLANYI, KARL

1957 *The Great Transformation: the Political and Economic Origins of Our Time*. Boston, Beacon Press.

REW, ALAN

1975 "Without Regard for Persons: Queueing for Access to Housing and Employment in Port Moresby." *Development and Change*, 6:37–49.

ROHLEN, THOMAS P.

1974 *For Harmony and Strength*. Berkeley, University of California Press.

ROYAL COMMISSION

1969 *Report of Royal Commission Respecting Radiation, Compensation and Safety at the Fluorspar Mines, St. Lawrence, Newfoundland*. St. John's, Government of Newfoundland.

ROYAL COMMISSION

1973 *Report of the Royal Commission to Enquire into the Amount of Social Assistance Received by Frederick and Ruth Thompson of Bauline Line, St. John's*. St. John's, Government of Newfoundland.

RUBIN, VERA

1962 "The Anthropology of Development." In Bernard H. Siegel (ed.), *Biennial Review of Anthropology, 1961*. Stanford, Stanford University Press.

SCHAFFER, BERNARD

1972 *Easiness of Access: a Concept of Queues*. Brighton, Institute of Development Studies at the University of Sussex (IDS Communication 104).

SCHAFFER, BERNARD

1975 "Editorial." *Development and Change*, 6:3–11.

SCHUTZ, ALFRED and THOMAS LUCKMANN

1973 *The Structures of the Life-World*. Evanston, Northwestern University Press.

SCHWARTZ, RONALD

1974 "The Crowd: Friendship Groups in a Newfoundland Outport." In Elliott Leyton (ed.), *The Compact: Selected Dimensions of Friendship*. St. John's, Institute of Social and Economic Research, Memorial University of Newfoundland.

SCOTT, ROBERT A.

1969 *The Making of Blind Men*. New York, Russell Sage Foundation.

SCOTT, ROBERT A.

1970 "The Construction of Conceptions of Stigma by Professional Experts." In Jack D. Douglas (ed.), *Deviance and Respectability*. New York, Basic Books.

SHOKEID, MOSHE

1971 *The Dual Heritage*. Manchester, Manchester University Press.

SILVERMAN, DAVID and JILL JONES
1973 "Getting In: The Managed Accomplishment of 'Correct' Selection Outcomes." In John Child (ed.), *Man and Organization*. London, George Allen and Unwin.
SILVERMAN, F. N.
1974 "Radiological Aspects of the Battered Child Syndrome." In Ray Helfer and Henry Kempe (eds.), *The Battered Child* (second edition). Chicago, University of Chicago Press.
SMITH, DOROTHY
1974 "The Social Construction of Documentary Reality." *Sociological Inquiry*, 44:257–68.
SMITH, M. G.
1960 *Government in Zazzau*. London, Oxford University Press.
STATISTICS CANADA
1973 *Census Tract Bulletin. Population and Housing Characteristics by Census Tracts: St. John's*. Ottawa, 1971 Census of Canada.
STEELE, B. F. and C. B. POLLOCK
1974 "A Psychiatric Study of Parents who Abuse Infants and Small Children." In Ray Helfer and Henry Kempe (eds.), *The Battered Child* (second edition). Chicago, University of Chicago Press.
STEINMETZ, SUZANNE K. and MURRAY A. STRAUSS (eds).
1974 *Violence in the Family*. New York, Dodd, Mead.
SUDNOW, DAVID
1965 "'Normal Crimes': Sociological Features of the Penal Code in a Public Defender Office." *Social Problems*, 12:255–76.
SUTTLES, GERALD
1972 *The Social Construction of Communities*. Chicago, University of Chicago Press.
SWARTZ, MARC J.
1968 "Process in Administrative and Political Action." In Marc J. Swartz (ed.), *Local Level Poltics*. Chicago, Aldine.
SZWED, JOHN
1966 *Private Cultures and Public Imagery: Interpersonal Relations In a Newfoundland Peasant Society*. St. John's, Institute of Social and Economic Research, Memorial University of Newfoundland.
TAUB, RICHARD P.
1969 *Bureaucrats Under Stress: Administrators and Administration in an Indian State*. Berkeley, University of California Press.
TURNER, VICTOR
1974 *Dramas, Fields, and Metaphors: Symbolic Action in Human Society*. Ithaca, Cornell University.
VAN STOLK, MARY
1972 *The Battered Child in Canada*. Toronto, McClelland and Stewart.
VAN VELSEN, J.
1967 "The Extended-case Method and Situational Analysis." In A. L. Epstein (ed.), *The Craft of Social Anthropology*, London, Social Science Paperbacks.
VOYSEY, MARGARET
1972 "Official Agents and the Legitimation of Suffering." *Sociological Review*, 20:533–51.
WADEL, CATO
1973 *Now, Whose Fault is That? The Struggle for Self-Esteem in the Face of Chronic Unemployment*. St. John's, Institute of Social and Economic Research, Memorial University of Newfoundland.
WEBER, MAX
1958 In H. H. Gerth and C. Wright Mills *From Max Weber: Essays in Sociology*. New York, Oxford University Press.

WEBER, MAX
1964 *The Theory of Social and Economic Organization* (edited by Talcott Parsons, and first printed in 1947). New York, The Free Press.

WEINGROD, ALEX
1966 *Reluctant Pioneers*. Ithaca, Cornell University Press.

WESTON, J. T.
1974 "The Pathology of Child Abuse." In Ray Helfer and Henry Kempe (eds.), *The Battered Child* (second edition). Chicago, University of Chicago Press.

WILLNER, DOROTHY
1969 *Nation-Building and Community in Israel*. Princeton, Princeton University Press.

WILSON, THOMAS P.
1970 "Conceptions of Interaction and Forms of Sociological Explanation." *American Sociological Review*, 35:697–710.

WOLF, ERIC
1966 *Peasants*. Englewood Cliffs, N.J., Prentice-Hall.

WOLF, ERIC
1973 *Peasant Wars of the Twentieth Century*. New York, Harper Torchbooks.

WORKMEN'S COMPENSATION BOARD
1974 Annual Report of the Workmen's Compensation Board, Newfoundland and Labrador.

ZALBA, SERAPIO R.
1971 "Battered Children." *Transaction*, 8:58–61.

ZIMMERMAN, DON
1969 "Record-keeping and the Intake Process in a Public Welfare Agency." In Stanton Wheeler (ed.), *On Record: Files and Dossiers in American Life*. New York, Russell Sage Foundation.

ISER Publications

Papers